MASSIVE TRAFFIC

208 Ways to Drive Hundreds or Even **Thousands** of Visitors to Your Website Within The Next 24 Hours or Less

ED RIVIS

MASSIVE TRAFFIC

ED RIVIS

First paperback edition printed 2010 in the United Kingdom
A catalogue record for this book is available from the British
Library.

ISBN 978-0-9558312-2-5

Published by Strategic Web Profits Ltd.
UK Freephone (0800) 612 0616
International +44 (0)1377 267365
http://www.StrategicWebProfits.com

Printed by the MPG Books Group in the UK

This book is dedicated to my Mum & Dad.

Table of Contents

Introduction

Since 2006 I've spoken to more than 3,000 small business owners, at seminars and Workshops around the U.K., these are both my own customers and clients and those of other organisations. Talking with the delegates in the live Q&A sessions and coffee breaks that followed, two things became apparent.

Firstly, that *most small business websites get very little traffic*, despite the business owners having spent thousands—or even tens of thousands—of pounds on them. Secondly, it appears that most people think driving traffic to their website involves Search Engine Optimisation [SEO], which means implementing a range of strategies and tactics to get a website to appear at the top of the Search Engine results. It's true, SEO *is* a very powerful traffic tactic. For example if you sell Widgets and on average 1,000 people a search Google for the phrase 'Widgets', and your web site appears at the top of Google's results, then of course that should generate a fantastic amount of website traffic. However, the search engine optimisation industry is *fiercely competitive*. It can take a *lot* of time and effort to achieve a first page ranking, and there are *no* guarantees. Other companies are constantly vying to get to the top of the search engine results, and when they do, everyone else gets pushed down. *Worse*, Google and the other search engines are liable to change their 'algorithms' at any time, meaning you could be at the top of page one today, and nowhere to be seen the next. So, in my experience there are *much* faster, quicker, easier and in many respects cheaper and more reliable ways of driving massive amounts of traffic to any website.

Take *traditional advertising* for example. I regularly run adverts in business magazines, and those adverts routinely send hundreds of visitors to my website each time they run. They sometimes send more than a *thousand* visitors, depending on the month and publication. It's highly effective, and yet I'm in a tiny minority of business owners using print ads to *deliberately* drive traffic to their website. Hopefully after reading this book you'll consider giving it a go too.

Then there are *strategic alliances*, or joint ventures as they're also called. My first ever strategic alliance generated more than £100,000 of extra revenues for my web design business, and that happened after just one short telephone conversation with one of my suppliers. It was easy to arrange, and in this book I'll give you loads of ideas on how you too can set up highly profitable alliances. Then there's *article marketing*. I'll give you an example of how a client of mine generated more than 15,000 enquiries by submitting free articles for publication on websites visited by her potential clients. Also very effective.

And... well I could go on, but I'll save it for the main section of this book, which reveals 101 tactics, plus more than 107 additional resources and links (more than 208 ways in total) to get more visitors on to your website. Read the short summary of each tactic, decide which ones to implement... *then get busy driving traffic!*

However, two quick words of caution:

1) *Traffic is vanity, conversion is sanity!* Driving millions of visitors to a website isn't going to do you any good if it then fails to do a good job of 'converting' those visitors into customers, enquirers or subscribers.

2) *Don't try and do everything yourself!* While it's important you know which traffic tactics are relevant to your business, and that you know how to perform each tactic effectively, I recommend you find *other people* to perform them, or at least some way of automating them. As a business owner you should spend most of your time *working* **on** your business, *not* **in** *it.*

In a nutshell, there's *absolutely no reason at all* why your website should not be getting anything less than **massive traffic**, and I hope this book helps you achieve that.

Wishing you every success,

Ed Rivis

Ed Rivis, August 2010.

P.S. Make sure you're signed up to my email newsletter at www.EdRivis.com for regular updates on how to use all these traffic tactics with *great* effect.

The #1 Most Essential Tip For Anyone Wanting More Traffic

A 'Call to Action' is a statement that asks your prospects to *do* something specific, like *visit your website* for example. Anywhere you advertise or promote your website, I suggest you also include a call to action. However, where most people go wrong with their call to action is that they just say "Visit our site" and then give their web address. Unfortunately that's just about the most *in*effective call to action possible! Far better is to give prospective website visitors strong, compelling and original *incentives* to entice them to your website. You could ask them to visit your website to download valuable free information, or to claim a discount or bonus, or something else that has a 'high perceived value'.

Whatever your call to action is, make sure it's of great interest to your target audience, and make sure you mention it everywhere you list your web address. Each of the 208 traffic tactics covered in the pages that follow all present the opportunity to prominently feature a strong call to action.

Examples include…

- "Visit www.website.com now for a XX% discount. Offer valid until dd/mm/yyyy"

- "Download our free report '7 Ways to do X, Y and Z' from www.Website.com"

- "Visit www.Website.com for the widest range of Widgets. Free next day shipping with every order."

- And so on.

Use these 208 traffic tactics in conjunction with a compelling call to action, and you should start getting more traffic than most websites in your industry.

Key Concepts

I'm going to liberally use the following phrases throughout this book, so I thought it'd be a good idea to explain what they mean before we go any further.

LANDING PAGES are the first page a visitor arrives on (lands on) when they visit your website. The homepage is a common landing page, but in theory *any* web page on your site is a potential landing page, as people click on to your site from the search engines, other websites, and links in emails.

LEAD PAGES are a special kind of landing page that ask visitors for their email addresses—and possibly first name and other details too—in return for **free** information. I use lead pages to offer my books and special reports for free, in return for a name and email address. Then I'm able to communicate with that website visitor in order to nurture a relationship. Most, if not all the traffic tactics in this book work very well when they're used in conjunction with lead pages. For example, your press releases could include a web address that take prospects onto a lead page instead of your corporate homepage.

CONVERSION RATE is the percentage of website visitors who respond to your web site by either buying enquiring or subscribing (whatever your website's trying to get them to do.) The average conversion rate for most small business websites is less than 3%, meaning less than 3 in every 100 visitors convert. One of the reasons for such a poor conversion rate is that they're using *inappropriate* traffic tactics. For example, a management consultancy who want more clients based in and around the London area aren't going to benefit from 1,000 website visitors from America. And yet many small businesses who want their website to generate enquiries from local businesses or consumers are spending time and money on traffic tactics that mostly get International traffic! *Hopefully after reading this book it will become apparent which tactics will attract the **right kind** of visitor to your website.*

TARGETED TRAFFIC refers to traffic that contains a high percentage of people genuinely interested in what you sell, so you get a good conversion rate (as explained above). All of the tactics featured in this book can get a lot of visitors to your website, but the only ones you should spend your time and effort on are those where a high percentage of the people they send to your site are *genuine prospective customers or clients*. The trick is to work out which they are!

QUALIFIED PROSPECTS refers to the 'quality' of traffic any of these tactics send to your website. A low conversion rate indicates the traffic tactics are producing *unqualified* prospects, resulting in poor sales and enquiries.

CONTENT is a key factor that determines online success. Good quality content in the form of the written word, or audio or video can attract visitors to your website like moths to a flame. *Quantity* of content is important too. As a rule, the websites that provide the most free information get the most traffic. Examples of those include *Google, YouTUBE, Amazon* and the *BBC* websites are all good examples. Also, websites with more content are favoured by the search engines, so you may notice that most of the traffic tactics in this book rely on lots of good quality content in one way or another.

BAIT & SWITCH refers to the practice of setting up a website that offers free information and advice, getting other websites to link to it on that basis, and then when the site's getting a decent stream of traffic suddenly replacing all the free content with an email subscription form. Everyone who visits the site from that point on will only see the email subscription box. Big email lists can be built using Bait & Switch, but as you can imagine, many people consider this traffic tactic to be Black Hat. Whether you use this or any other tactic in this book is, of course, entirely at *your* discretion.

The 208 Traffic Tactics

In this book there are *more than* 208 possible sources of website traffic—places you can go and things you can do, to get more visitors coming to your website. Read them, and decide which are most appropriate for your business—and the type of people you're trying to attract to your website. When you've done that, all that's left to do is *implement*... actually start working on the tactics—or even better, delegate them to other people, *so you get more traffic without lifting a finger.*

Here they are.

Submit articles

Article Marketing is a form of *content syndication*, which means offering your own material—written articles, audio or even video content—for publication on other third party websites and in traditional media like newspapers, magazines or even T.V. and radio.

Article Marketing is a very powerful way of driving more traffic to any website, and best of all, it can be performed *without any cost whatsoever*. It can be as simple as writing an article of between 400 to 500 words, and then offering it to other website owners and publishers to use on their website. They get free content to keep their audience engaged, and you get people reading your name and clicking the link in what's called the 'resource box' at the end of the article and arriving on your website. *And voila!* **Instant, free, and highly targeted traffic.**

> I say 'highly targeted' because you'll only get people clicking the link at the bottom of your article if they were interested in what you wrote about, the topic of which should relate directly to the content on your website they click through to.

A colleague of mine submits articles to sales and marketing websites. A percentage of the people who read her articles click the links in them, and end up on her website and subscribe to her email newsletter. As a result she's built up a very large email subscriber list (database) of sales executives. She's now able to email them and offer her own range of products and services, and has won lucrative sales training contracts as a result. And it all starts with short articles of between 400 – 500 words in length.

How To Write and Submit Articles

Performing article marketing is as simple as researching and submitting articles to publications and web sites which are read and visited *by your target audience*. However, one key point to always remember when article marketing: Articles are *not* sales letters. They are usually unbiased "How to" articles that give the reader some useful information. The only part of the article that can 'sell' is the last one or two paragraphs, which are what we call the 'Resource Box' or 'Author Bio'. In that you can—depending on where the article's published—have a *call to action* which suggests the reader clicks a link through to your web site 'for additional information'. It's crucial the resource box doesn't just talk about you the author, but also offers them *additional information*, like a free report on the same subject as the article itself.

Use Article Submission Services

An easy way to submit articles is to get someone else to do it for you! With article submission services you simply give them the article, and they do all the laborious submissions for you.

Examples of such services include:

- www.SubmitYourArticle.com
- www.ContentSpooling.net
- www.UniqueArticleWizard.com
- www.iSnare.com

Use Article Submission Software

Rather than logging in to individual directories to submit your articles you could instead use software that automates (or at least semi-automates) the whole submission process. Examples of software you could investigate include...

- Article Submitter Pro (www.ArticleSubmitterPro.com)

- Article Announcer (www.ArticleAnnouncer.com)

Submit to Tutorial Sites

Tutorial websites are a type of site that offer 'How to' articles, and are some of the most highly visited sites online today. If you can find tutorial websites in your industry, offer your articles and other content for publication and reach out to an audience of highly targeted prospects.

Write a Newspaper Column

A client of mind writes for her local newspaper, who publish her advice each week in the form of a short column. Each week, her prospective customers and clients read the column and without realising it are automatically revering her as the 'go to' expert in her industry. *Unfortunately when I first met her she'd already been published for years, but not one of her articles had a resource box with a link to her website or a call to action. Don't make the same mistake!*

Are there any opportunities for *you* to become a columnist in a local or national newspaper? It may only take a quick phone call to find out.

Write for Industry Publications

If you operate in a niche industry, and your articles wouldn't be relevant in 'mass-market mediums' like newspapers, then you could instead write and submit articles to industry specific publications. People who read those would be highly-targeted prospects for your products and services.

Submit Guest Articles

Even if you're not a regular contributor to a publication, you could always contact them and offer an article they can publish as a 'one off'. Your only requirement would be for them to include your resource box at the end of your articles, which of course includes a web address and a call to action.

Form strategic alliances

Strategic Alliances, or *Joint Ventures* as they're also called, are one of the most powerful ways of getting new traffic to your website, in a very short space of time and at very little or even *zero* expense. In fact, you could start by approaching **friends and colleagues** whose customers and clients are similar to the type of people you sell to. Those are usually going to be the quickest and easiest alliances to establish. (My first alliances was with a supplier who had also become a close friend.)

It should also be fairly easy to establish alliances with **suppliers** you've had a long and happy relationship with. **Complimentary trade partners**, who sell *different* products and services as you, but to the same type of clients, also make ideal candidates. And if you implement a formal referral system you could get your **existing customers and clients** acting in a strategic alliance capacity too.

Finally, you could even approach your **competitors** and agree to promote each other to your *lapsed customers and clients*. It would be win/win for both parties. (At the time of writing I've just done an alliance with a company who could be considered my competitor, but we were both happy to refer each other to our lapsed customers on the basis we had nothing to lose and everything to gain.) That kind of arrangement may be welcomed by your competitors too. Try it and see. You should both get a lot from it.

Once you've decided *who* to form an alliance with, you then need to decide *how* to reward them, and also how to actually *do* the promotion. Let's look at some ideas.

Swap Advertisements

You could both agree to put adverts on each others websites and 'share the traffic'. Visitors on their website see and click your advert, and vice versa.

Swap Lists and Exchange Traffic

You could both agree to email your lists and recommend each others websites. (And if your strategic alliance partner has a much larger email list than yours, then you could simply arrange for him or her to email the same number of people as you have on your list, or vice versa.)

Co-registration Opt-ins

You could set up a web page that asks for the visitor to submit their name and email address in return for *two* free gifts, from both you and your alliance partner. You could even share the cost of promoting the offer. Then when the visitor submits their data it's automatically added to *both* yours and your alliance partner's email database. (NB: The web page should mention that the visitor will be added to the mailing list of both you and your alliance partner.)

For a Favour

In just a few short months a friend of mine built a list of more than 30,000 prospects, by simply asking nine of his friends and colleagues to promote his website to their email lists. They agreed to do it, not for commission, but *as a favour* to be repaid in the future. In other words they can come back to him at some point and ask him to promote them to his email list. He's quite happy with that.

*Who do **you** know, who has a large email list, and who you know well enough to ask them for a favour?*

For a Commission on Each Action

You could pay your alliance partner for each action that results from them promoting you to their database. That action could be a sale, subscription, enquiry or opt-in… whatever you both agree on.

Swap Tweets

If you and your alliance partner both have a sizeable following on *Twitter* (www.Twitter.com), you could simply agree to tweet a promotion to each others lists. This is called a *Tweetswap*, and is quick, effective and again doesn't have to cost anything. You could even arrange to do it on a regular basis.

Swap Autoresponders

Autoresponder swaps are when you add a new email to your autoresponder sequence with the promotion for your alliance partner, and they do the same for you. This is a great way of promoting each other, because it's a 'set it and forget it' type arrangement—very easy to set up and run on an ongoing basis without any sweat whatsoever!

Strategic alliances are without a doubt one of the fastest ways to grow your business today. *I wish you the best of luck in setting them up and getting amazing results.*

Send direct mail

Use direct mail and other printed literature to encourage prospects and existing customers or clients to visit a web site with a call to action. Where other advertisers will simply say "visit our web site for more information"… be very specific about the action you want people to take when they get there. For example, 'Visit www.Example.com and download our free report which reveals X, Y and Z'.

Once a letter has got someone onto a lead page, which in turn has got them to sign-up, the cost of ongoing communications with that new prospect has been significantly reduced.

Driving customers to a lead page via direct mail or print advertising is sometimes cheaper than gathering them online…and it's scalable. Cross-marketing with direct mail can boost your return on investment by up to 500%, and have the same effect on your website traffic too.

Update your brochure

A good brochure will not only list the features but also explain the benefits of your products and services. However, it also presents a great opportunity to prominently display a web address with a strong call to action. Also, given that it's advisable and good practice to send out a covering sales letter with your brochures, that sales letter also presents another great opportunity for a web address with a strong call to action.

Create a Brochure Specifically for your Website

In addition to updating your existing corporate brochure, you could create a brochure with the *specific goal* of increasing your website traffic. I did this recently with a brochure whose sole purpose was to drive traffic to my seminar website. On every page the brochure prominently featured the web address, with a call to action asking the reader to 'reserve a seat' my next live seminar. Response was excellent.

Figure 1: Brochure specifically designed to drive traffic to a website.

Mail out tear-sheets

Tear-sheets are written and printed to look like articles that have been torn out from a real magazine or newspaper. You can send them to prospective customers with a 'J' note (a Post-It note that says something like, "I thought you'd be interested in this, best wishes, J.")

Since the tear-sheets look like genuine articles, they carry more weight with the public than advertisements do because the media and reporters are seen as unbiased third parties. The purpose of your tear sheets could be to direct people onto your website, where they then subscribe, enquire or buy whatever was featured in the tear sheet.

Negotiate a reader offer

Instead of paying for ad space in magazines and newspapers you could try and negotiate a reader offer with the publication. This is where you offer their readers something special—a free gift or big discount. The publication wins by being seen to be making special offers available *for the benefit of their readers*. And you benefit by getting **free ad space**—which can of course include a link to your website. A web address to a *landing page* could be one of the ways readers respond and request their free gift or claim their discount.

Buy a TV spot

Although television advertising is usually expensive, and mainly used for brand and image enhancement or special deals, it can still be used for website traffic generation, with potentially amazing results. For example I heard that American web hosting and domain registration company *GoDaddy,* paid a *lot* of money for a television spot that ran during the American Super Bowl—but the advert generated traffic which resulted in *millions* of dollars of revenue!

Now while you have an opportunity to target particular audiences, according to what programmes they watch, with television advertising you're competing with other advertisements, and viewers' ability to switch channels to avoid your advertisements. If a prospect sees your web address in a television advert they'll have to remember it until they're next on their computer. So, make it easy for them—ensure your domain name is short and memorable. Consider registering a separate domain name just for the TV advert, that way you know *exactly* how much traffic it's generated.

Advertise on the radio

With radio, you have a highly targeted audience. Find out which radio stations your prospects listen to, and choose which programmes you want your advertisement to be attached to. Since people often listen to the radio while driving (and therefore can't jot down your contact details), you again need to have a memorable web address and an enticing offer.

Alternatively, rather than paying to advertise on a radio station, you could instead promote your products and services indirectly, by offering to be interviewed on subjects you're an expert in. People who listen to that will be exposed to you, and also, hopefully, you'll get a chance to mention your web address during the call too.

Run adverts in print publications

Running adverts in print is a massively overlooked way of getting website traffic, *if* done correctly. It's one of the four key tactics I use for driving traffic to my websites, and I strongly suspect it could be one of yours too. The key is to *run adverts that don't look like adverts!* Your adverts should look more like editorial content, like the main articles and features in the publication you're advertising in. Why? Because most people buy print publications to read the articles and features, *not to look at the adverts!* It's a really important point.

Also, make your adverts promote *one* thing, and one thing only. Don't dilute your adverts with lots of different offers. And definitely **prominently** display an easy to remember and easy to type web address so it's easy for people to respond.

Your adverts could run in newspapers and magazines you know your target audience read, and could appear in any format from an expensive double page advert down to small line advertisement where you pay by the word or letter.

I frequently run full page ads in business magazines which cost thousands of pounds. It's possible you first heard about me by responding to one of those adverts. However, I only do so because I *know* they produce a return on investment. What I'd recommend though, is that your first attempt at using print ads to drive website traffic is done on the small scale. Start with a small inexpensive classified and line ad. If you get a profitable response from those then you can start to scale up.

There are three really critical aspects to advertising in print...

1) **Only advertise if you can track the response.**

   All my print ads have their own web addresses so I know *exactly* how many people have responded.

2) **Only spend as much money as you can afford to lose!**

   An old mentor taught me that phrase. I always keep that in the back of my mind when running new adverts!

3) **Use landing pages and lead pages.**

   Never advertise a web address that sends people to the home page of your main web site. (That's what most advertisers do, and it's incredibly ineffective in most cases because homepages are so cluttered and full of distractions that it significantly lower response.)

My **MASSIVE TRAFFIC X4** video training programme covers traditional advertising in print in a *lot* more detail. I explain how to track print ads scientifically, how to get conversion rates up to as high as 98%, and give you a raft of proven print ad layout templates you can easily edit.

Visit **www.MTX4.com** for more information.

Run classified ads

Classified advertisements mainly appear in print material, such as newspapers, magazines and trade journals. Such advertisements are usually text only, and consist of a headline, body copy (the words that fill the main part of the advertisement) and contact details. Such advertising can be very easy to set up and is extremely profitable when the full lifetime value of sales-leads acquired that way are fully realised.

Figure 2: My first ever newspaper line ad.

N.B.: I recommend you don't advertise your main web site, because you'll never know whether your advert produced any visits and sales. Instead, I recommend you register new domain names (web addresses) and create specific *landing pages* for your classified ads. That way you can track response and monitor whether your classified ads are generating profitable traffic or not.

Online Classified Advertising

You could run some test ads in the online classified directories like www.CraigsList.org. You could even add a Classified Ads section *to your web site*, to generate extra revenue and increased traffic from both advertisers and readers.

Advertise in cinemas

If customers are being asked to spend a lot of money then they probably need a fuller explanation of benefits than is possible during an average-length advertisement. However, if you sell a product or service that is easy to explain and has mass-market appeal then it could be well suited to cinema advertising.

A cinema advert that ends with a short, memorable domain name, supported with a strong call to action could produce a useful stream of extra traffic to your website.

Sponsor a charity

Charities often have high-quality domains. Become a sponsor and you may be able to get a link placed on their site back to yours. Search engines will see and like those back-links, and of course visitors to the charity website may see and click the links to find out more about you.

Also unlike a normal paid link, those types of links can remain posted long after the donation is made. And what a *great* way to build your website traffic—by supporting good causes!

Public relations

With good *public relations* you can gain free exposure to thousands of readers, listeners and viewers. Also, media coverage, or publicity, has a major advantage over paid advertisements: Articles written by a journalist carry more weight with the public than advertisements do, because the media and reporters are seen as unbiased third parties.

The challenge is that the media are not interested in your business or your products, but they *are* interested in useful information supplied in an attention-grabbing way. If you supply them that information, they'll give you exposure. However to get regular exposure in the media you need to learn how to write an effective media release that catches attention and compels a journalist or radio or TV presenter (or, more likely, their production staff) to call you for more information.

To create web traffic from publicity, you need to give the media a compelling reason to write or produce a story that *drives readers directly to your website*. Once they're on your website you can close-the-sale or enlist visitors into an automated follow-up process.

To grab the media's attention and create web traffic using publicity, you can use tactics such as sending press releases, pitch letters, or media kits (online or offline), staging publicity events, writing articles for printed magazines, trade journals or newspapers and blogs, ezines, or article directories or by providing controversial feedback on a current story.

Phone your prospects

Get your telesales team to call prospects, and while on the phone, get them to visit your website. Reasons could include an online demo, or to get them to sign up to a free email newsletter, or claim a discount and so on.

Train staff to ask for email addresses

The larger your email database, the more traffic you get when you broadcast emails, so it's advantageous to train your staff to ask everyone they come into contact with for permission to subscribe them to your email newsletter.

Media inserts

Inserts are promotions carried in a newspaper or a magazine that are not part of the scheduled design. They may be stapled, folded, glued or simply placed inside the pages of the magazine or newspaper.

Magazine or newspaper inserts are a powerful way for companies to distribute information to a wide range of customers. They can be used to introduce a new product, publicise a special promotion or even kick off an advertising campaign. Just about every type of business can use inserts. Inserts come in all shapes and sizes, often contain coupons or samples, and help the advertiser present his/her message. It may also cost less to distribute brochures or catalogues by inserting them, than it would be to mail them.

Your insert must attract your readers' attention and compel them to take action, for example to visit your lead page and sign up.

One common objection I hear to inserts is that "nobody reads them". That's quite interesting to me. I can only assume the people who say this have never actually tested putting an insert in publications read by their target audience. Either that, or their inserts were ill conceived. I say this because every time I run inserts in publications read by my target audience, I never fail to generate hundreds of new enquiries.

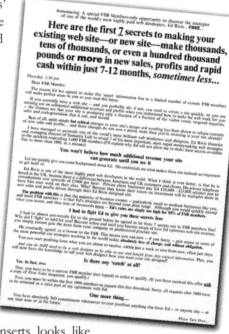

The secret is to make your inserts look interesting, and *not just like another advert*. My most successful inserts looks like nothing more than a plain letter typed in black and white and printed on an A4 sheet of paper. (Figure on right).

Payroll and invoice inserts

By special arrangement, your web site promotions could appear on media inserted into other companies payroll slips. Always take the opportunity to promote a compelling offer that gets noticed and makes people want to visit your site. Remember, a web address on its own, will do very little.

Piggy-back Inserts

Approach other companies who send direct mail to people who are your kind of prospects, and ask if you can insert your promotions inside their mailings. If they say yes (maybe because you pay them for each insert, or perhaps a commission on the response you get) then those inserts could feature your web address and be automatically driving more traffic to your website.

Become a sponsor

By sponsoring ezines or newsletters, content sites, online events or chat sessions, you can achieve great exposure for your own site. Sponsors might donate money, web development, web hosting, web site maintenance, or other products and services to web site owners in exchange for advertising on their site.

The benefits of sponsorships on the Internet are that you can target a specific audience, you usually get 'first call' on banner ad placement, and you show your target market that you care about their interests. Overall, by sponsoring other sites on the Internet, you have the opportunity to get directly in the face of your target market and channel more traffic on to your own website.

Advertise on billboards

The advantage of outdoor billboards is that the advertisements are often large and in prominent positions, so they attract lots of attention. If people are passing the same way every day, they see them over and over again.

Billboard messages must be *brief* and *memorable*, since people usually only see the billboard for a second or two. Long domain names that are hard to spell or remember probably won't work very well. Consider registering short memorable web addresses specifically for billboard adverts.

Also, as it's impossible to target your message to a specific audience, you'll need to appeal to a diverse audience to get worthwhile results.

Finally, billboard advertising isn't cheap, and in some places where there is high traffic volume you'll need to book well in advance, so make sure you track and test results to ensure you get a good return on investment.

Human signage

One of my suppliers started a company that sold T-Shirts with funny messages on the front. He managed to get a celebrity to wear one of these T-Shirts on two major television programmes, which resulted in a surge of web site traffic.

Wearable promotional gifts like baseball caps and rugby shirts can have your company web address emblazoned across them.

Face to face

If your company has a lot of face to face meetings, perhaps there's an opportunity for those meetings to increase your website traffic. Maybe while your sales person is sat with the prospect, they could walk the prospect through your website and explain the benefits of using it. At the very least they could leave reference material which encourages future website visits.

Business cards

Maybe it's just me, but just think how many times you've been handed a load of business cards at a seminar or exhibition and thrown them in a drawer and never see it again until the day you clean the drawer out. Then it goes straight in the bin! (Possibly because you've forgotten who gave you the card in the first place!) With this in mind, the weakest thing you can put on your business cards is just your web address alongside your name, job title, company logo and address.

A far more powerful technique for getting website traffic from your business cards (and the resultant increase in sales and enquiries) is to use one or even both sides of the card to display a compelling offer for valuable free information that can be accessed from your website. Those kind of cards will stand out head and shoulders above the other cards your prospects are given.

Advertise on public transport

If you know your target audience uses public transport on a regular basis, then paying for poster advertisements that appear on buses and trains obviously makes sense. However, be aware that these kinds of advertisements are like outdoor advertisements—you're paying for a generic mass-market advertisement, in the hope that you'll appeal to a specific audience. Your message and call to action need to be absolutely clear and hugely compelling to get response.

Vehicle signage

If you're aiming your product or service at a local market, use signs promoting your web site on your company vehicles. Make sure the web address is memorable. People may only see it for a second or two.

Send Promotional gifts

Offer a range of practical and attractive gifts that carry your web site address and a strong call to action. These gifts could include mouse mats, mugs, pens, badges (if you have a membership site), book markers, T-shirts, waterproof jackets, baseball caps, bags, umbrellas, even golf balls. Make them practical so that the recipient uses them (and sees your web site) often.

Approach clubs (or start one!)

Approach clubs or groups with offers that will be of great interest to their members. Or, start your own club and add the members' area to your website.

Update your company stationary

Place your URL and a compelling call to action on every business, marketing and advertising piece you produce— whether its invoices, fax cover sheets, complimentary slips, business cards, flyers, brochures, press releases or pamphlets. Put your URL on your letterhead as well and include it in your logo design if possible. And remember, having a call to action next to your URL will greatly boost the number of people who respond and visit your site.

Broadcast faxes

Fax broadcasting involves sending a document or documents to many recipients simultaneously. Documents that need to be sent to a large audience, such as announcements, press releases, newsletters, or other types of information, are often sent by broadcast fax. Some businesses routinely send conference or workshop registration reminders, invoices, and other materials using this form of communication. Whatever communication you send, consider adding your web address and a strong call to action.

Going a step further, a colleague of mine uses fax broadcasts to promote a free gift that can be acquired by simply going to a web address. His fax is *completely* handwritten and looks like a 'note to a friend'. He gets a *staggering* level of traffic from those broadcasts.

CAUTION: Although advertisements can also be sent via this method, be aware that the U.S. prohibits unsolicited advertisements, also known as 'junk faxes'. The U.K. has laws too, so be sure to check before pressing the send button.

Broadcast SMS messages

Apparently more than half the world's population has a mobile phone now, which makes SMS broadcasting a key marketing vehicle. You can reap big rewards from mobile marketing if it's done right, by sending out relevant, interesting or useful messages people actually want and enjoy receiving. Each message you send out could include a web address, along with a compelling call to action of course.

Broadcast voice messages

Voice broadcasting is a mass communication technique that broadcasts a pre-recorded message to hundreds or thousands of recipients. It's even possible to personalise the messages using text-to-speech software.

In terms of website traffic generation, your voice broadcasts can suggest listeners visit your website to claim valuable free information, or to make an enquiry or buy a product or service.

Flyers

Place your web address, along with a compelling call to action, on any flyers you use to promote your products and services.

Yellow pages & phone book adverts

Consider making your web address appear more prominently in your Yellow Pages adverts. Include a compelling *call to action* and you could easily double or triple the amount of enquiries the adverts generate.

Fairs, festivals, trade shows and exhibitions

To maximise your involvement in industry fairs, festivals, trade shows and exhibitions, consider offering people you meet there a compelling reason to give you their contact details and to go to your website. Don't just hand over leaflets or brochures—most will be discarded. Give people a compelling reason to hand over their contact details to you. Consider holding a contest or offer free CDs, DVDs, online videos, etc., and mention that everyone who enters the contest or requests the free gift will be signed up to your free email newsletter.

Video marketing

Creating promotional videos and uploading them to video sites like www.YouTUBE.com and www.Viddler.com has become a very popular traffic tactic. The basic idea is to create interesting and entertaining videos that also include references to your website, either mentioned in the video itself and/or overlaid as a graphic on top of the video. In theory, a percentage of the people who watch your videos will be impressed enough to then visit your website for further information.

However, in the process of writing this book I wanted to give you an example. So I went onto www.YouTube.com and decided to find videos uploaded by management consultants (an arbitrary decision for no particular reason other than I thought the videos that appeared would make great examples). *I was wrong!* The first video to appear *was* professionally produced, and very well edited. It was shot using two cameras (so two different camera angles), and it had good quality audio, which is essential if you want your videos to be professional. But the video I watched was totally and utterly boring! I'd give you a link to it, just to show you an example of the type of videos *not* to create and upload, but I won't so as not to offend the company who uploaded it. However what I *will* do is give you the number one reason that made is such a weak attempt at video marketing. Basically, it was all about *them*, the company being featured in the video. How long they'd been in business. The type of people they employ. And why, in *their* opinion, *they* feel they're the best management consultants, bar none! Like I say, *incredibly boring*, and I can make an informed guess that it has produced exactly *zero* enquiries for them.

What if, instead of making that chest-thumping, self-aggrandizing video, they made one that gave their prospective clients some *useful ideas and interesting insights* on how to overcome a common managerial challenge? Possibly using one of their existing clients as a case study of how to successfully overcome said challenge. Now that video *would* be interesting to a manager facing the same challenge. And it would also automatically *position* the management consultancy as experts, *without them having to say it themselves*. Bear this in mind when brainstorming content ideas for your own video marketing pieces.

Shooting your Video

Professional video cameras can cost up to £20,000 or more. Thankfully, you don't need to spend anywhere near that amount of money to shoot your marketing videos. In fact, you may not even need a camera at all. You could just create 'screen capture' videos—recording of your computer screens as you perform various tasks on it or run a Powerpoint presentation. (Check out *Camtasia* from www.Techsmith.com.) Or, if you *do* want to shoot live video, you could use inexpensive video cameras like the *Flip* (www.TheFlip.com) and other modern camcorders which can shoot in the new high definition format, and make it very easy to transfer the recordings to your computer and onto the web via 'Flash cards'.

Uploading Your Video

When you've created a great marketing video, you'll need to upload it to as many video sites as possible, to maximise exposure. Also with each video upload you'll need to specify keywords that identify the subject matter covered in them. Those keywords are important because they'll allow people interested in the topic of your videos to search for and find them, both on the video site and also in the search engines. (Video submitted to popular sites like www.YouTube.com can appear in the search engines a lot faster than say content you add to your own website.)

Uploading your videos is relatively straightforward. You could visit each video site where you want to publish them, create an account and login, upload your video, and provide any additional information about you, the publisher, and about the content of it. *But that's the hard way!* The easy way is to take advantage of video uploading services that allow you to upload the video to them, and then their service automatically uploads your video to all the major video sites without you having to lift a finger. Examples of these services include www.TrafficGeyser.com and www.TubeMogul.com.

When you upload videos you should also consider promoting them in your social networking community sites and forums, as well as on your blog and website.

Broadcast live video

Probably one of the more well known video streaming services is www.uStream.tv. A few colleagues of mine have used this service with great effect over the last year or so. It may work very well and be a great way of building your website traffic too.

Google Adwords & PPC

Google Adwords text advertisements are the small adverts that appear down the right hand side of Google after you've performed a search. In my opinion Google Adwords is *one of the most powerful advertising facilities in the world*, because you *only* pay when prospects respond to (i.e. click) your adverts. This is totally unlike advertising in print, where you usually pay 'on speculation', *regardless* of whether anyone actually responds or not.

Even better, *Adwords traffic is **fast** traffic*. Literally within 15 minutes of setting up a campaign you can start getting highly targeted visitors onto your web site and buying from you. *It is quite simply one of the most **instant** and immediately effective advertising mediums in the world.*

Figure 3: Google Adwords text adverts on www.Google.co.uk

Google are constantly improving and enhancing the features offered by the Adwords system. For example they now allow you, the advertiser, to use *placement targeting*, which means that your ads can appear on the sites most likely to have an interest in your products, services, and content. You have the option to select your sites based on their subject matter, demographics, even specific URLs (web addresses), gender, or even based on their income level and age group. Narrowing your target audience in this way can be highly effective.

Based on how you decide to advertise, you can select between cost per image (CPM) or cost per click (CPC) pricing. I generally prefer the latter, but it's possible you get better results with CPM. It depends on your industry and your offer, and whether your goal is to generate sales or enquiries.

To sign up go to www.Google.com/Adwords.

As complex as the service is, Google have made the process fairly straightforward, so provided you're moderately technically competent you shouldn't have any problems. Also once you're signed up you'll be able to browse their online help and training resources, but BE WARNED! Google make money *when people click your adverts*, so their training is primarily focused on *helping you get as many clicks as possible*. However, that may *not be in your best interest!* There's no guarantee that the people who click onto your website will buy from you, so you need to do a number of things to optimise your conversion rate and ensure you get as many sales from your Google Adwords clicks as possible.

These additional considerations include…

- Turning on *Conversion Tracking*—which is an extra feature that tells you which keywords are most profitable for you.

- Having as many *'negative keywords'* as possible—which are words and phrases which *prevent* your adverts from showing. For example an accountant who specialises in giving tax advice could specify the word "free" as a negative keyword. Then their advert would *not* appear to anyone who searches on the phrase "free tax advice".

- Optimising your *landing pages*—which are the web pages people arrive on when they click your adverts. Your landing pages need to do a good job of getting the visitor to take action, be it to buy, enquire about or subscribe to whatever it is you're offering. You can have the best, most optimised and efficient Google Adwords advertising campaign in the World, but if you've got a poorly designed landing page then it's all a waste of time.

- *Split-testing* your text adverts is a key factor in whether you can beat your competitors with Google Adwords. It basically involves writing *more than* one advert for each AdGroup. The Adwords system then automatically displays them in rotation as people search on your keywords, and once enough people have seen and clicked your adverts Google then tells you which is the best performing advert. In my experience most new Google Adwords advertisers fail to split-test, and as a result are paying too much money per click.

- Systematically *monitoring conversions* is another essential factor in ensuring your Google Adwords advertising generates a good return on investment.

- *And there are many other factors beyond these.*

Google Adwords is such a complex service I think the best advice I can give you—to ensure you don't lose your shirt—is to seek professional help, or pay an agency to do it for you, (although that has it's own risks attached!)

Without this turning into a sales pitch I'd encourage you to checkout my **MASSIVE TRAFFIC X4** training programme, where my 'live screen capture videos' will show you how to set up and run *highly profitable* Google Adwords campaigns. Visit **www.MTX4.com** for more details.

Other Pay-Per-Click Services

There are hundreds if not thousands of relevant websites that you can run paid advertisements on. Your text ads should send people to your lead pages—never to your main corporate business or e-commerce site, unless you have the ability to carefully track whether those adverts are producing a return on investment. *Examples of these sites include:*

- www.LinkWorth.com

- www.Miva.com

- http://searchmarketing.yahoo.com

- https://adcenter.microsoft.com

- www.AdBrite.com

- *And many, many others.* A search on Google for the phrase 'Pay Per Click Advertising' should yield lots more for you to test.

Pay Per Lead

Pay Per Lead (PPL) is a form of affiliate marketing where you pay your affiliates based on the conversion of leads, such as a file or software download, completion of a sign-up form for a newsletter, trial offer sign-up, or other desired action. If your website visitor has arrived on your site by clicking a PPL affiliate link, and completes the required action in accordance with the affiliate agreement, you pay your affiliate. Search on Google and the other search engines for the phrase "pay per lead" and you'll get active links to lots of PPL programmes you can test.

Pay Per View & Adware Networks

As the name implies, *Pay Per View* is online advertising where you pay a fixed sum each time your advert is shown to visitors. Some of the most well-known free content websites in the world support this advertising mechanism, whereby when visitors go to read the free content, before it appears they're exposed to an advert for a specified period of time, after which the free content appears.

An alternative PPV mechanism involves web surfers *voluntarily* installing '*adware*' software on their computer, this gives them access to website content they'd normally have to pay for, but which is free because they've agreed to install the *adware* software. Then, the *adware* software automatically monitors the sites they're visiting and displays relevant adverts—and the advertisers Pay Per View.

Some people misunderstand this traffic tactic and think that the *adware* software installed on the end-user's computer is unethical or even illegal. However, end-users choose to install the *adware* so they gain access to premium content for free, meaning that this traffic tactic is 100% legitimate. The only downside is that traffic can be very low quality—there's no guarantee the people viewing your adverts are qualified prospects or not. With that said, you *can* get massive traffic—and get a lot of viewing your web pages for a *very* low cost.

At the time of writing there are quite a few PPV services you can test. Enter the phrase "Pay Per View" into your favourite search engine for a current list of publishers to advertise with.

Start an authority site

Establishing an *authority site* is a valuable way to increase your marketing reach, gain status as a recognised expert and *get more traffic*.

To see an example of an authority site check out www.EdRivis.com.

Notice how it 'personally brands' me, and without explicitly saying it, positions me as an expert. Also note how the main thrust of the site is on giving free advice and information, which is a *key indicator* of an authority site, as opposed to sites that only provide information about the products and services for sale.

Good authority sites typically have hundreds (or even thousands) of pages of valuable content, in a variety of formats and styles. This is a major attraction for visitors. *Traffic to your web site will increase greatly when you're considered an authority.*

Authority sites are recognised more quickly by search engines because they have high volumes of inbound and outbound traffic, and they also have a large number of inbound and outbound links to relevant sites. They achieve high ranking on search page results with search engines.

If you start one, the most important thing about your authority site is to ensure that you regularly update it with relevant, unique, fresh and high quality content. Your content must be updated frequently since search engines are searching for organic growth of your site through consistent addition of new pages of content, and relevancy of all links.

If you sell complex products or services, consider establishing separate authority sites, and cross-pollinate traffic between them.

How to Set up an Authority Site

My own site at www.Edrivis.com was created in one afternoon. Or at least the 'empty shell' of the site was created that fast. It's taken a few years to add the hundreds of article and videos, but of course you've got to start somewhere, so if you'd like an authority site like mine here's how...

1) **Register a domain name** (web address). You could opt to go down the personal branding route like I did, and use your name. Or you could instead use a domain name that alludes to your expertise. At the time of writing www.AjaxWhois.com is a great free service I use to quickly research domain names.

2) **Set up some web hosting.** (Check out my web hosting review site at www.swphosting.com for my current recommendations.)

3) **Add** *Wordpress* to your web space—it's free software you can download from www.Wordpress.org that puts you in charge of the content (articles) on your website, without needing to resort to a web designer each time you want to add something new.

4) **Upload a theme** (another word for 'design'). There are loads of free themes available for *Wordpress*, simply Google the phrase "free Wordpress theme" and you'll find a few thousand or more to choose from! Or do like I did and pay for a more sophisticated theme. (In this latter case you can Google the phrase "premium Wordpress theme".) I decided to go for a theme that looked more like a magazine, on the basis I was creating an authority site.

You can at this point start tweaking the site, by adding what are called "plug-ins", but that's just polish. You're already in a position to start posting content to your new authority site. All of the other tactics in this book can be used to start driving traffic to it—but I can tell you from experience that a nicely designed authority site with lots of great content will *automatically* attract and generate some very interesting opportunities for you.

Start blogging

A *blog* is any site that displays content in the form of diary entries, or 'posts' as they're called, in reverse date order. They also allow readers to add their own comments underneath each post. In other words, blogs are a type of 'community' web site, and as a result can get more traffic than traditional 'corporate' websites. (In fact many corporate websites have blogs added to them as a way of building brand loyalty.)

These days it's easy to create a blog and doesn't have to cost anything. Again, *WordPress* (www.Wordpress.org) is easy to use software that enables you to create, run and maintain your blog. It's free, relatively easy to install, and contains dozens of powerful facilities you can leverage as you become a more proficient blogger. What's critically important is that you download and install the software on your *own* web site. Or start a new web site that's entirely a blog (as a stand alone entity.)

Host Your Own Blog

I recommend you *don't* let a third party company host your blog under *their* own domain name—your traffic will be going to their website instead of your own!

On your blog, display links to your main company web site, your landing pages, and also any other web sites relevant to the topics you'll be discussing. Make it a resource that people will want to visit regularly.

When you add a new page to your website, mention it in your blog. Whenever you post an entry in your blog, always make sure that you link it back to your site. You can also create more than one blog, and link them all to your main business website.

Make friends with other blog publishers and get links from them too.

Pinging And Feeding Your Blog Content

When you post a message in your blog, your blog software should automatically send a ping to the main blog search engines such as *Technorati*. Services such as Google's www.Feedburner.com allow your blog feed to be distributed easily to your site's users. They also allow email subscription of your feeds. Some people will visit your blog to read it. Others will use an RSS reader on their computer or a web-based service such as *MyYahoo*.

Tagging and Social Bookmarking

Tagging is a powerful driver of highly-targeted traffic. Webmasters and Bloggers label or 'tag' their content with the most relevant keywords. Then websites like *Technorati* use those tags so people can find your blog easily.

You create content and label it with relevant tags. Then, visitors who like your page, bookmark it using a service like http://del.icio.us or www.Digg.com, which then counts the bookmark as a vote for the quality of your site. The more votes you get, the higher your page ranks in their search results. This has already become a powerful driver of highly-targeted traffic. People who achieve a good ranking for a popular tag, report getting 10,000 new visitors a day! And, as bookmarking grows in popularity, the quality of the results and the number of people using it for search increase exponentially.

Blog owners provide a choice of social networking and social bookmarking links or graphics at the end of their articles. Using a tagging service like *Technorati* attracts people to your blog. You label your blog with a tag and any *Technorati* user who has subscribed to that tag will be notified each time you make a post on your blog about that subject.

Social bookmarking sites allow you to share your bookmarks publicly, tagging them to enable others to find them. If people who visit these sites decide your pages are worth sharing, they'll bookmark and tag them so that other people can find them.

You can also share an RSS feed of your bookmarks. When you add a bookmark, they learn about it automatically.

Third Party Hosts

Now although above I recommend you host your blog on your own domain (web address) rather than on someone else's website, I still recommend you take advantage of the third party blogging sites like...

- www.Blogger.com

- www.Wordpress.com

- www.Typepad.com

Those and other services like them allow you to register for a blog which they host on *their* domain. You post articles to them just like your main blog. However, the purpose of those third party hosted blogs is to send traffic to *your* main blog, website and lead pages. The goal is to ultimately get the email address of people who find you on those sites so you can then filter them onto your main websites. In addition, blogs hosted on the third party sites will give you a useful opportunity to quickly get more search engine result boosting back-links.

Become a Guest Blogger

Providing *other* bloggers with your articles, which they can post for free on their blog, is a great way to increase your website traffic. Those articles will not only increase market awareness of your personal brand—and position you as an expert—the people who read them may click your link and arrive on your website. Some may even 'Google you' to see what comes up. (Hopefully it's your site that appears at the top of Google's results for your name and/or brand!)

There are two ways you can get 'guest blogging gigs'. The first is to wait for someone to contact you and ask if you'd write an article for them. To increase the likelihood of being invited to write for a third party blog, research your market and find the most influential bloggers then make a point of commenting about their posts on your blog and send them the links. Referenced parties may even promote the fact that they've been featured or quoted. As a result, they might link to your content directly, reciprocate the favour or invite you to be a guest blogger.

The second way of getting guest blogging gigs is to actively seek guest blogging opportunities. Make sure you keep an eye on the main blogs in your industry and jump on the opportunity whenever they announce they're looking for guest bloggers. Or take the initiative and contact them to see if they'd like you as a guest blogger. Just one short article of 400 words could provide you with a lot of back-tracking traffic to your website if the blog you appear on is very popular.

Look For Guest Bloggers

Instead of you being a guest on someone else's blog, ask them to be a guest on yours! Many of the people who appear as a guest on your blog will give their own email subscribers and blog readers a link to it. When they do, *you get their traffic!*

Look For Guest Editors

Ask experts within your market or industry to be 'guest editor' for a week (or other length of time—you decide). It can be as easy as you sending them a few vetted emailed questions and asking them to provide answers, which are then formulated into content.

Comment on other people's blogs

Commenting on blogs related to your web site theme or industry is another way of getting free traffic. When you comment, most blogs allow you to also provide your name and web address. Other people who read your comments are then able to click your name to go to *your* website. So for example let's say you sell golf equipment. You could comment on golfing blogs run by celebrities, golf courses and even other golf equipment retailers. People who read the blog you comment on will obviously be interested in golf, otherwise they wouldn't be reading it. Therefore, if they see and read your comment and click your link out of interest, you will have just successfully funneled another unique visitor, hopefully a qualified prospect, from that blog to your own blog or website.

Commenting on blogs also creates back-links to your site, which can aid your efforts to rank higher in the search engines.

However, I recommend you don't comment just for the sake of creating back links. That's called 'link spam', and is frowned upon in the internet community. Only comment when you have something valuable to add to the discussion.

That said, one key approach to making this tactic work for you is to be one of the *first* people to comment on a blog when a new post appears. That way more people will see your comment, rather than it being comment number 104 of 106,

47

so only the last few people see it. To make sure you're one of the first to comment you could add yourself to the blogs RSS feed and get an alert each time a new post appears. Then quickly go and be one of the first to comment.

How to Find Popular Blogs to Comment on

Finding blogs to comment on is easy. There are 'blog search engines' you can use, which include…

- http://blogsearch.google.com

- http://technorati.com/

- Any search engine—simply search on the phrase '{topic} blog', replacing the word 'topic' with whatever's relevant to your industry. So our golf shop example could search for phrases like 'golf blog'.

At the time of writing this book Google's blog search facility is reporting 39.5 Million results for 'golf'. That should be enough to keep someone busy commenting and seeding links back to their golf website for quite a while!

However, bear in mind that Pareto's Rule will probably apply to the blogs you comment on. Probably a lot *less* than 20% of the blogs you comment on will send you *more* than 80% of the unique visitors who come to your sites from the comments you leave. So, if you start performing this tactic I recommend you keep an eye on your web analytics package. Monitor which blogs send you the most traffic over time. Those could be the blogs you frequent and comment on more in future.

Podcasting

Portable On Demand Broadcasting ('Podcasting') is a widely used technology which involves a collection of digital media files being distributed over the internet, typically for playback on portable media players and computers.

People can subscribe to your 'Podcast' broadcasts via RSS feeds and automatically receive them. If you create your own informative, useful podcasts, you can reach a whole new audience.

Podcasts enable you to put a voice with your site and your product, and create a stronger bond with your visitors. You can present fresh new ideas on your niche product using audio and video media—enhancing both the value and the appeal of your niche products. It is a much more active approach to reaching your audience versus the passiveness of a blog. The combination of blogging and podcasting create a dynamic marketing strategy for your market.

You'll need to get your podcasts listed in podcast directories such as www.Podcast.net and on www.iTunes.com. Make sure you use an eye-catching title to grab the attention of people scanning the directories.

Submit press releases

Submitting press releases *online* can serve two purposes. Firstly to promote your offer, and secondly to help your search engine optimisation efforts by getting more back-links to your site. Here are some examples of places to submit press releases online:

- www.PRWeb.com

- www.PRWebDirect.com

- www.SourceWire.com

- www.PressReleaseMonkey.com

Submit Press Releases Directly to Journalists

As well as submitting press releases through online services you could also go the traditional route of submitting your press releases direct to journalists. My friend, public relations expert Paul Green did that, and managed to get 1 Million visitors to his clients website in less than one week, and that was from submitting a single press release to one journalist!

Make Yourself Available For Media Interviews

Being interviewed as an expert will increase your website traffic. American marketers should look to create a media profile on www.HelpAReporter.com, and here in the United Kingdom, create a profile on www.ExpertSources.co.uk.

Testimonials

You can attract or 'catch' more clients by collecting testimonials from your customers and using them in your marketing materials (both online and offline). It lets your customers do the talking and convincing for you and your business. If possible, include the customer's photograph, their real name, position within their company and location. That way, prospects can see that the testimonials are genuine. Ask customers to go *into detail* about how the product or service has improved or benefited their lives.

Testimonials not only help to build trust in your company, add believability to your product claims, and provide social proof, but can also attract large amounts of highly-targeted web traffic. They help to increase your keyword density, which can help your search engine ranking. Comments from customers are also a great way to discover popular new keywords. You should use testimonials in all your marketing material: your advertisements (classified, Google Ad Words, banners, etc.), autoresponder messages, lead pages, sig-files, articles, press-releases, viral eBook, RSS feeds, and blog posts.

Now with all of this said, probably one of the biggest opportunities for using testimonials to generate traffic is *you* giving other people testimonials. If you've had a great experience with a product or service, send the vendor a great testimonial, and be sure to have your name **and web address** at the bottom of the testimonial. (Just take a look at the back of books in your industry to see how many have endorsements which end with a name and web address!)

Another way of increasing the likelihood of your testimonial being used is to create multimedia testimonials (audio or video recordings) for people to display on their sites. Of course there's nothing to stop you subtly working in a mention of your product and give a link back to your website, but do it too obviously and it's likely your testimonial will get discarded and be seen as an very obvious attempt to snag traffic from the person you're giving the testimonial to.

Amazon and other Commerce Sites

You can also submit testimonials on web sites like Amazon. Providing the site doesn't disallow them, testimonials and endorsements you submit could all have links to your websites.

Get celebrity endorsements

Celebrity endorsements carry enormous impact. Marketing expert Dan Kennedy says celebrities dominate every aspect of the media and every demographic therefore "celebrity-ising your business is NOT an option." *(In other words it's mandatory!)*

There are multiple ways you can quickly and easily "celebrity-ise" your business. But why should you? For a start, they make it possible for you to charge premium prices and fees and sell at prices significantly higher than your competitors or the industry norms without having to make any changes to your product or service, advertising, marketing or sales. That boosts your income.

Celebrity association reduces your need to buy advertising and lowers your overall costs of acquiring customers. There's abundant evidence that adding celebrities to advertising, increases readership, listenership and viewership, thus making each pound you invest produce more.

Celebrity endorsements also means you can get more and better word-of-mouth advertising or 'buzz', and therefore more referrals. All of which will almost certainly show itself in the form of increased website traffic.

Start a content website

A content site simply means any website where the focus is on providing useful free content, and because of this, content sites can get a lot of traffic.

You can benefit from content sites in two ways. Firstly you can start your own (checkout www.EdRivis.com as one such example of a content site that also doubles up as an Authority Site). Secondly, the people who visit content sites could be highly targeted prospects for you, if the subject matter of the content site relates to your industry. So, if the content site supports advertising (many do), placing some strategic advertising on them could be a great source of traffic.

Run live events

Running live events like seminars, workshops and conferences can not only position you as an expert, but also becomes a great source of increased website traffic.

In 2009 I started running my own live events in the form of seminars (www.WebStrategyLive.co.uk) and workshops (www.WebProfitWorkshops.co.uk) and I've noticed this boosts my website traffic in three ways. First, when I announce my events (using primarily emails, but also direct mail and social media channels) I get increased traffic to my websites on the back of the 'buzz'. Secondly, delegates who attend my seminars and workshops visit my sites more, following my live events. And thirdly, I'm able to talk about the live events in the days and months following them. I can then also give my other email subscribers, customers and clients links to content generated at the events themselves.

Also, I haven't done this yet, but getting other companies to sponsor live events can also increase traffic if they also agree to promote the events and their promotions contain links to your website.

Speak at other people's Live Events

You could also start speaking at other people's live events to gain wider exposure for your company. Although it may not be possible to 'sell from the stage' you may be able to promote your web site or landing page in the promotional literature.

Run webinars

The single most effective selling medium is face-to-face and the online medium that most closely resembles face-to-face selling is *webinars*.

Webinars (also known as e-seminars, webcasts and teleclasses) can be either live or pre-recorded (called "On Demand Webinars"), and enable you to reach potential customers using a presentation with audio instead of visuals or content alone. Webinars work because they are perceived by prospects and customers as providing content. They can be a great source of new leads.

To ensure webinars boost your website traffic you can ask people who want to join you on your webinar to register in advance, by giving you their name and email address. Therefore in future you'll be able to send them emails with links back to your site. Also during the webinar you can give people links to your websites and web pages relevant to your presentation.

Run teleseminars

Teleseminars (also called *conference calls*) are nothing more than phone calls with dozens or hundreds or even thousands of people on the line listening in, as one or more presenters talk about a specific subject. The presenters can also invite listeners to ask their own questions in open 'Q&A' sessions.

People love information, especially if it's free. You can advertise your free teleseminar and have people register through your lead page. You can then capture the names and email addresses of people who have expressed an interest in the topic or product that you will be speaking on. This provides you with a ready source of valuable leads as the people who are committed enough to take time to listen to your teleseminar have demonstrated their interest in your product or service.

Your lead page should say something like, "Give me your first name and primary email, for free, instant access to the teleseminar phone number and pass code." After someone gives you their details you can give them the information for the call, and thank them for subscribing.

Offer 'On-demand' Teleseminars

Record your live teleseminars and offer them as recordings for download or live streaming from your website... yet another great way of encouraging more people to visit your website.

Co-present Teleseminars

If you're invited onto other businesses teleseminars as an expert, you'll hopefully get the chance to give listeners a link to your website where they can get more information. (Offer a free report or information product if you want to maximise the traffic you get from that.)

Co-host online or live events

Boost your exposure by hosting online or live events with other businesses. Do it to gain credibility, potential customers and—by prominently displaying your web address at every opportunity—more website traffic.

Offer reviews

If you're well known and respected in your industry you could start to offer to review other people's products and services on your website or blog, either free or for a fee. Not only can this be an extra source of income, it could also be a great source of extra website traffic, as the business whose product or service you review, email *their prospects* with a link to the review on *your* website.

Surveys & petitions

Conducting surveys and petitions on your site can generate extra traffic, not just when your own customers and prospects take part and come to read about the results, but also through the word of mouth that can be generated about it. For example I blogged about a survey I ran a while ago, and published the surprising results. Then another blogger commented about my survey results on his website and linked to my blog post. That automatically resulted in extra traffic as his blog readers clicked through to read my survey results.

Use the online auction sites

Auction sites such as eBay are not only great places to buy and sell products and services, they are also somewhere to find quality visitors for your web site. That's because auction shoppers are in the mood to buy and expect to see a 'sales pitch'.

The key to getting traffic from auction sites is learning how to funnel the auction sites' customers to your own web site without contravening their rules and regulations.

Here are four ways to funnel traffic from auction sites:

1. Sell or give-away eBooks with links to your site.

2. Post your web and email address on auction pages.

3. Partner with other auction sellers.

4. When you sell products on auction sites, include with the product literature that encourages your customers to visit *your* website. Offer them the chance to download free information like User Guides, make special offers and offer discounts and promotions on items related to what they bought.

Get leverage on the Shopping sites

Becoming a merchant on shopping sites allows you to do a similar thing as with auction sites. Offer your products on those sites and benefit from their massive traffic. Customers who buy your products on those sites can then be incentivised and channelled on to your own website.

For example:

- www.Kelkoo.com
- www.google.com/products

Run banner ads

Banner Ads are small advertisements that are placed on web pages. Companies usually develop their banner ads, find sites for 'banner ad placement', and then either purchase or *trade* banner space.

Banner ads can create awareness of your web site and increase the traffic to it. They should be placed on the sites that your target market is most likely to frequent, thus encouraging them to click through and visit you. They can be placed on search engines, content sites, advertising sites, portals, and online magazines.

Web traffic analysis software can tell you the next day if the banner ad is working or not by tracking the number of visitors who clicked through and visited your site as a result of your banner ad the previous day. This provides you with the opportunity to change the site on which you are advertising or to change the banner ad to see if it attracts a greater audience.

Test the banner exchange networks

Banner Exchange Networks are a group of website owners who agree to show each others graphical adverts (Banners) on each others websites. Traffic can be extremely low quality, but for your industry it may be worth running some tests to see how much mileage you get from this tactic. To get a current list of networks, search Google for the phrase 'Banner Exchange Networks'.

Test the traffic exchanges

Traffic Exchanges are groups or 'communities' of website owners who agree to look at each others websites, in return for credits. If you join an exchange, the more websites you look at, the more credits you earn. The more credits you earn, the more *your* website is visited by other people in the exchange.

Most exchanges work on a 'credit ratio', which tells you how many websites you need to view in order to gain one visitor to your website, and many exchanges also offer an 'upgrade' option to level out and create a more equal credit ratio, and almost all exchange networks are free.

The main thing to bear in mind with traffic exchanges is that the person looking at your website will only be visiting it for a very short space of time (usually 20 – 50 secs). For this reason it's advisable to send them to a *lead page*, where visitors can quickly submit their name and email address in return for valuable free information. (At which point you have their email address and are then able to offer them your products and services by email.)

For a current list of active traffic exchanges, type phrases like 'traffic exchange' into Google, but please note… I recommend you *don't* spend any money on traffic exchanges until you know you're getting a return on investment. Traffic exchanges may increase the number of visitors who see your website, but may not necessarily increase the number of sales you make! As with all traffic tactics, *test carefully* to ensure you—or whoever you delegate— generate a return on the time you invests in participating.

Offer an RSS feed

RSS, which is an acronym of the phrase 'Really Simple Syndication', and it is a relatively new way of delivering content to your prospects and customers or clients. Unlike email, which may or may not successfully get delivered to the people you send it to, due to things like Spam filters, RSS is a *guaranteed way of ensuring your message gets delivered* to the recipient, every time, without fail. RSS can also increases your website traffic by improving search engine rankings, generating traffic from RSS specific sites and getting your content published on other sites. Each of these activities can generate new website visitors, which can then be converted into subscribers with whom you can communicate via both RSS and email.

There are many ways to start offering RSS feeds (as they're called) to subscribers. One of the easiest is to build a website using one of the common blog software scripts like *Wordpress* (www.Wordpress.org), which comes with built in RSS feeds. Then every time you add new content to your website, the RSS feed is automatically updated for anyone subscribed to it, and that could result in people clicking links in your RSS feed and ending up on your site.

Start advertising in third party RSS feeds

In addition to offering your own RSS feeds to increase traffic, you could also pay to insert adverts in the RSS feeds of *other* companies, whose RSS feed subscribers are your ideal prospects.

To find RSS feed publishers who support adverts, search Google for phrases like 'RSS advertising network'. The search results that come up will include companies like *Pheedo* (www.Pheedo.com), who rather than being an RSS feed publisher themselves, are instead giving you access to a network of publishers across a wide range of industries.

Advertise on CPA networks

A Cost-Per-Action (CPA) Network is a group of professional marketers who've agreed to promote products and services in exchange for a commission. These 'networks' are essentially a collection of 10,000 to 100,000 active affiliates. They usually have their own affiliate manager and affiliate tracking software.

While the most common type of action is Pay-Per-Sale, you'll also find some networks offering Pay-Per-Lead. The leads often cost less because they only require a visitor to provide contact information such as phone number, email or mailing address.

By using CPA Networks, you can start generating online sales in as little as 48 hours with very little work and absolutely no risk. Be aware that there may be set-up charges.

With CPA Networks your ability to create traffic is directly related to how many network members decide to promote your offer. Since affiliates only get paid per-sale, their main concern is how well you convince visitors to make a purchase. The higher your conversion rate and visitor-value, the more network members will actively promote your product or service to their audience...and the more sales you will produce.

Advertise in ezines & newsletters

Ezine advertising—which means running adverts in other peoples email newsletters—can be a very cost-effective way of driving massive traffic to your website. Unlike newspapers, ezines are not restricted to a geographic area and, unlike magazines that cover broad topics, ezines are extremely focused.

Due to their highly specialised nature, ezines provide the perfect opportunity to instantly connect with a large group of web users interested in a specific topic, and get in front of people who are highly targeted prospects.

Ezine publishers are trusted by their subscribers. They have built reputations for being in touch with their readers needs and have proven that they can deliver timely information that their readers can actually use to solve their problems, meet their needs, make them look better or feel better, and answer their questions.

Getting an advertisement into the hands of those people who are looking for a product or service that will solve their problem will drive them to your website in search of it, if your product or service fits the bill.

Instead of merely advertising your website or an affiliate product, send people to a page where you offer a free report or mini-course in return for their email address.

Advertising in ezines is far less competitive than most other advertising methods. Ezines are almost always archived and people frequently refer to past issues of ezines when they are searching for information.

Advertise on Facebook

Facebook, one of the most heavily trafficked websites in the world, now has an incredible advertising facility. You can write an advert that speaks specifically to your target audience and decide whether to pay 'per click' (only if people actually clicked your advert) or 'per thousand impressions' (charged a fixed price for showing the advert 1,000 times regardless of how many clicks your ad gets).

Facebook allow you to specify a wide range of criteria that determine to whom your advert displays.

You can show your adverts to people based on their location...

2. Targeting

Location

Country: [?]   United Kingdom ×

○ Everywhere
◉ By City [?]

Enter a city

☑ Include cities within 50 ▼ miles.

You can show your adverts to people based on their age and other demographic criteria...

Demographics

Age: [?]	18 ▾ - Any ▾
Sex: [?]	◉ All ○ Men ○ Women
Birthday:	☐ Target people on their birthdays
Interested In: [?]	◉ All ○ Men ○ Women
Relationship: [?]	☑ All ☐ Single ☐ Engaged ☐ In a Relationship ☐ Married
Languages: [?]	Enter language

Based on their likes and interests...

Likes & Interests

Enter an interest	[?]

Based on their education and workplaces...

Education & Work

Education: [?]	◉ All ○ College Grad ○ In College ○ In High School
Workplaces: [?]	Enter a company, organization or other workplace

You can even show your adverts to people based on what other Facebook connections they've got.

Within a few minutes of making those selections you can post the advert on Facebook, and once it's approved—usually within a few hours or less—the advert will start running, drive traffic to your website and hopefully generate either sales-leads or actual sales if that's your goal.

Of course, you still need to make strong offers and write adverts with compelling 'direct response style' copy, otherwise it's all just a waste of time!

Caveat: I've tested Facebook advertising and have so far *not* found it to be particularly effective for advertising B2B products and services. However, testing continues, and I do know that businesses which sell consumer products are having a field day with Facebook advertising at the moment! Probably because it's still relatively knew unlike Google Adwords which is saturated with competition in most industries.

It may be worth at least testing Facebook advertising to see what results *you* get. To start using this, go to Facebook and log in to your account (or create one if you're not already on Facebook.) Then click the 'Advertising' link at the very bottom of the screen.

Run paid ads on forums

Some forums support paid advertisements. If your industry has some very popular online forums that support paid ads they could become a source of highly lucrative traffic.

Use the Product Launch Formula

The *Product Launch Formula* (PLF) is an online training programme that explains an entire system for not only generating high-volumes of traffic but also for selling huge quantities of your products within a *very* short time frame, thanks to the power of psychological sales tactics like 'scarcity' and 'reciprocity'. It's beyond the scope of this book to explain the whole system. The best place to learn it of course is to enrol on the proper course. Unfortunately at the time of writing this book you can't enrol on to the PLF training course—the doors only open every 3 or 4 months (sometimes longer). However, if you go and sign up to their waiting list then the next time they start recruiting students you'll be under no obligation to buy the programme, but you *will* be privy to some of the most excellent free training available on the Internet. Visit www.swplf.com to sign up to Jeff's waiting list.

Get leverage on information products

Information products are either online or offline (physical) reports, whitepapers, books and audio or video recordings that people can read, watch or listen to. If you're an expert you can create your own information products. I call the process 'Shrink-wrapping your brain', and explain it in a lot more detail on my 'Shrink-wrap your Brain' website over at www.ShrinkWrapYourBrain.com.

Basically, the moment you capture (record) your knowledge in digital or physical format you're suddenly able to make it available as a shrink-wrapped product, either for free or as a paid product. There are some very compelling reasons why I suggest you Shrink-wrap your Brain, and generating website traffic is one of them.

Give away free video and audio recordings

Offer your prospective customers or clients a free DVD or access to a streaming video online in return for their contact details. The DVD or video must be about a subject they really want to know about, and related to what you ultimately want to sell them. When they request the CD or DVD, or sign up for online access to the audio or video recording, tell them you'll also add them to your email list, so in future they'll receive emails and click through onto your website.

Create and sell video and audio recordings

Instead of giving away video or audio to generate sales-leads and extra traffic, you could of course sell the information product instead. But don't forget, the packaging for your products is the ideal place to display your web addresses too.

Also, in addition to selling information products on your own sites, you could offer them on third party sites like...

- http://advantage.amazon.com (or .co.uk)
- www.EBay.com

- www.ClickBank.com

- www.PayDotCom.com

Submit *written* information products to ebook directories

If you've written an information product then you could submit it to the 'free ebook directories'. Search in Google for "ebook directory" and "ebook directories" and list your free ebook everywhere you can. *Make sure it's seeded with links back to your website!*

Build links

Link building is the process of deliberately seeking to increase the number of web sites that link to yours.

Getting other websites to link to yours is a powerful way of building website traffic. Most popular search engines use 'link popularity' and 'link relevancy' as part of their ranking criteria. The more links to your site, the more popular it is, so the number of links you have to your site can significantly impact your placement with those search engines. Also the more links you have to your site, the more opportunities search engine spiders have to find you, and links generally stay active for a long time so there are numerous advantages to link building.

There are three basic strategies for increasing the number of sites who link to you: first, you can actively seek link partners; second, you can distribute content that drives visitors to your site; third, you can attract links naturally by building a link-worthy website.

Link baiting is a process of putting valuable free content on your site that other website owners like so much they decide to link to it (from their site.)

A *link exchange* is when two companies who market to the same segment of the population but who market complimentary rather than competing products or services can help each other by exchanging links. The link exchange is free to both parties. Choose link exchange partners that have the highest *page rank* for their keywords. These are the sites that will have the most traffic and more people will see your advertisements and have the opportunity to click on your link, visit your website and, perhaps, buy your product or service and sign into your opt-in list, as well.

Manual Link Building

The most basic way of building links to your site is to contact the owners of other websites and suggest the link. Or, special link building software like 'Arelis' or 'Zeus' which can assist you in building links, and submitting press releases via online services, which will also build links to your site.

Automated Link Building

Services like www.3waylinks.net were created for the specific purpose of automatically building links back to your site. You could also take advantage of article submission services (mentioned in the section on Article Marketing) to automatically build back links.

Another fairly new service launched recently is *Wordtracker Link Builder*, over at www.wordtracker.com/linkbuilder. I haven't used that service yet, but it looks very good.

Get Trackbacks

Trackbacks are a quick easy way to create quality inbound links. All you do is read other blogs and make comments about them in your own blog. In your post include a *Trackback* link to the original discussion. This will automatically create a link to your blog from the original blog....which provides a way for you to steer a piece of their traffic to your website.

What's more, trackbacking increases the value of content on your site, by adding new perspectives, fresh information, and new ideas. It makes your site more interesting and interactive with other sites. Since you are connecting to other websites, it allows you to talk with other people without using email, forums, or other large discussion groups—it's quick and easy. You'll connect with more people, which can then lead to more potential customers and increased business.

Perform Search Engine Optimisation (SEO)

Search engines are one of the main ways people look for information online. They all operate in the same way. Someone looking for information enters a word or phrase and clicks a 'Search' button. The search engines then displays a list of web sites (called the 'search result') which it believes are most *relevant* to the phrase entered. (Relevancy is determined by a complex set of algorithms which vary from search engine to search engine.)

Getting your web site in the free ('organic') listings on the main search engines can propel your site from a low traffic, low revenue web site, into a money generating cash cow. The challenge is in getting it there! For most industries it can take a concerted effort over an extended period of time to get your website to appear on the top of the first page of results in search engines like Google. (And once your site *is* on the coveted first page of search results, it probably won't stay there for very long... *unless* you work on *maintaining* the first page position.)

It's way beyond the scope of this book to explain *in detail* how to optimise your website (change the words, images and links, and add more web pages and content) in order to get your site to the top of the first page results. What I can do though, is reveal the key factors that affect whether your site is going to appear high up in the search results or not...

1) **Get other web sites to link to yours**. Search engines like Google, look for sites with 'authority'—and the more external third party sites that link to yours, then the more Google will perceive your site as an authority in your niche. (See the other traffic tactics in this book on Authority Sites and Link Building for more tips.)

2) **Add content**. Then add some more! Search engines favour sites with lots of content.

3) **Links should contain keywords**. If you have a website that has widgets, and one of the pages on that website is all about purple widgets, then you should link to that page from other pages on your site, and from other sites around the Internet, with the wording of the link containing the phrase "purple widgets". Those links contribute to the way search engines score and determine how relevant the page is to the phrase 'Purple Widgets'.

Other factors include the domain name (web address) and how long the domain has been registered (i.e. how old your website is). How many visitors your site gets, how long people stay on the site, whether the site links to 'bad' websites, and hundreds of other constantly changing factors. (No wonder there's an entire industry of search engine consultants.)

More Ideas on How to Get Rankings

- Create one or more content web sites on themes related to your main products and services. On those sites have small text adverts that link to your main website, using relevant keyword text. (In other words build your own additional websites that link back to specific pages on your main website.)

- Start a blog and add as much quality information as possible, to give the search engines plenty to 'feed on'.

- Write articles and publish them on those sites and also as many other sites as possible.

- Invite other people (for example experts in your industry) to submit articles to appear on your own content sites and blog.

- Ensure each page on your site makes frequent mention of your main keywords. Ask the owners of other web sites to link to your information sites. If they do, then your sites 'link popularity' will improve, which in turn can improve your search engine rankings.

- Plus, many of the other traffic tactics in this book will *automatically* improve your chances of getting higher in the organic search results.

Beware the Black Hat!

Black Hat tactics are the 'frowned upon' tactics that some people do to try and get their sites ranked highly in Google and the other search engines.

An example of Black Hat SEO is having web pages that include large blocks of text that are white text on a white background. Visitors can't see the text, but Google can, and in the past these large blocks of text could be stuffed with keywords that meant Google would rank the site well.

Unfortunately that's now considered by Google to be a Black Hat technique, and any website that does it could be penalized or even completely banned from Google.

There are many other such techniques that can get websites banned from Google and other search engines, and I personally don't recommend or advocate Black Hat tactics in any way. Interestingly, there are still a lot of web marketers out there who think it's a viable way of increasing website traffic.

One thing I recently heard was how an SEO company routinely performs Black Hat SEO on their clients *competitors* websites, in order to get their client's site higher up the rankings. (When they manage to get their clients competitors site banned and removed from Google's results, their client's site automatically moves up a place in the rankings.) If that story is true then it means anyone who relies *solely* on 'organic' Search Engine traffic for their site is a sitting duck!

Viral marketing

This is the digital form of word-of-mouth advertising and is an easy way to spread your marketing message from person-to-person using the tools of the Internet. It's such a powerful technique because by using online tools such as email, people can communicate with everyone they know very, very quickly and it spreads exponentially at a grass roots level with no cost and no involvement by you.

The challenge is, that to 'go viral' you have to create something either totally outrageous or so unusual it starts the snowball effect. However, if you are able to do that, and craft a truly viral message, it'll result in a never-ending web traffic creation tool that drives tonnes of tightly targeted visitors to your website.

Create & distribute software

Creating and distributing computer software that contains links to your websites is another very effective traffic tactic. You could hire someone from www.VWorker.com or www.ELance.com to create the software. Once created you could get extra publicity by submitting your downloadable software to directories like www.Download.com

Start a user-generated content site

As the name implies, a user-generated content site (UGCS) is one where most if not all the content (text, images and multi-media) is created by the users of the web site. Most user generated content sites require some sort of registration before allowing users to 'post' content.

A startling fact about this is that the most popular websites on the web are nearly *all* UGCS sites! YouTube is a user-generated video site. Amazon allows publishers to upload book information and allows its customers to then rate them (all examples of user-generated content). And Google is a collection of user-generated content in that its results are a massive compilation of other website content! Nearly all the content on Facebook, LinkedIn and other social sites is generated by its members.

What opportunities are there for you to add user-generated content areas to your website? Or, maybe even start a brand new site where the focus is on entirely user-generated content.

Host an article directory

Add an article directory to your website and encourage your website visitors to submit their own articles. The advantages of hosting your own article directory are two-fold. Firstly, Google appears to like *industry specific* article directories and can rank them favourably. Secondly, your site can attract more traffic as a result of people visiting your site to post or read articles.

There are a lot of free and paid scripts you can download that allow you to quickly setup your own article directory. Google the phrase 'article directory script' to get a current list.

Get active on forums

Whatever your product or service, there is a specific group of people who are congregating online right now who are very likely to buy it. They're the ones who are gathered on blogs and forums discussing a topic for which your product or service *is an answer to their problem, challenge or issue.*

To encourage traffic to go from those forums on to your web site, add your comments to their forum postings. Be helpful. Provide free advice and information. And critically, with every post you automatically include your forum signature—three or more lines of text at the bottom of each comment you leave that includes a link back to your site.

A percentage of the people who read your forum comments and appreciate your advice will click the links in your signature and end up on your website. This is another great source of free, targeted traffic.

Host a link directory

It may sound complicated but a self-hosted link directory could be as simple as a normal web page that contains a list of links to other websites. If you already know how to create a basic web page, then you can create a link directory. If not, ask your web developer to set one up for you, it shouldn't cost much. Or, use link building software to automatically generate—and help you manage—a link directory. Even better, there is software and scripts that allow you to create self-service link directories where other people can add their own links, (as in 'self-service').

So why would you do this? Why allow other people to add their links to *your* website? Well, first of all, you'll get traffic as people go to your site to post their link. Secondly you'll get increased awareness from the search engines that not only like sites which have a lot of back-links, but also which have links to other (external) sites too. Finally, you can set up your link directory to require the person who wants a link in your directory to first add a link to your site from theirs. This way you automatically get more back-links, which are favoured by the search engines and may also get clicked by the other site's visitors too.

Start a forum/community site

Adding a forum or 'community area' to your existing website is a powerful way of benefiting from recycled traffic, and if you're seen to be the owner of a very popular industry specific forum, it can also enhance your credibility as an expert.

There are lots of free software scripts you can use to quickly get one up and running. The key thing to ask though, is *why* should people join your community? What's in it for them? If you can give people a strong enough reason to join your community site then it should do well, and generate a lot of traffic.

However, before you rush off to launch a community site, you first need to decide who is going to manage ('moderate') it? Moderating community sites can take a lot of time. Will it be you, or someone else? Also ensure you will have a way of enticing new forum members from your forum to your email newsletter or to the rest of your site. (A common way is to require forum members to register, and as they do so, indicate their preference to receive additional communications from you.) If you don't have any mechanism in place to get permission to contact forum participants beyond or outside the forum, they'll just take part in discussions and leave, using up bandwidth without generating any revenue for you.

Upload free content to directories

There are hundreds if not thousands of online directories that want you to upload your written, audio and video content to, for the benefit of their visitors.

Upload EBooks

Upload reports, whitepapers and e-books to document directories. Seed the document with clickable links (hyperlinks) to your website.

Upload Software

Create software that contains links to your website. Offer them on your own website and also if it's software you don't mind giving away free (or maybe even create it for the sole purpose of giving it away free) you can upload it to free software directories.

Upload Audio

Upload audio recordings to audio directories. Of course the audio will mention and give listeners compelling reasons to visit your website.

Upload Slides

Websites like www.SlideShare.com want you to upload your slideshows and presentations, again for the benefit of their visitors. So, create a nice useful, interesting (maybe even entertaining) slideshow on a subject relevant to your industry and target audience, and make sure the slideshow ends with a strong call to action giving a compelling reason for viewers to visit your website.

Start micro-blogging

Micro-blogging (also called 'nanoblogging') service allow users to send and post brief messages—usually just text—around 140 characters or less.

These text updates are displayed in the user profile page, and are also immediately sent to other users that have chosen the option of receiving them. The home user can send the message to everyone, or to a restricted list.

Current examples of micro-blogging services include…

- www.Twitter.com → hugely popular at the moment.
- www.Plurk.com
- http://Identi.ca
- www.Jaiku.com
- www.Tumblr.com

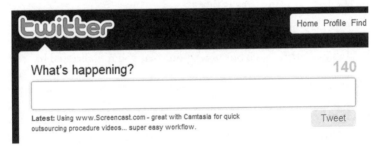

Figure 4: Tweeting on Twitter

As a way of driving massive traffic, your micro-blogging activity should first and foremost engage the audience so they enjoy and look forward to your messages. When you've got a loyal following, occasionally posting messages embedded with links to your website can generate potentially huge amounts of *instant* website traffic.

Create a Squidoo Lense

This used to be a very effective way of winning new website traffic. *Squidoo* is a free community website that allows you to create your own pages of website articles and links, which it calls 'Lenses', on subjects that interest you, and which relate to the products and services you sell. Other people can then view those pages... hopefully clicking the links on them and ending up on your website.

Visit www.Squidoo.com for more information, to create a free account, and also to search *Squidoo* itself for a digital tonne of information on how business owners and Internet and Affiliate Marketers are using *Squidoo* to increase their website traffic.

Become a Stumbler

StumbleUpon.com is a community website that allows users to bookmark, recommend and share websites they like with other 'Stumblers' (as they're called). The basic way it works is this...

1) Open a free account at www.StumbleUpon.com

2) Fill in a form to tell StumbleUpon what you're interested in.

3) Install the free StumbleUpon toolbar in your web browser.

4) Finally, click the 'Stumble' button in your toolbar and based on your preferences, it'll suggest websites that other people who share the same likes and dislikes as you, are recommending.

When a website appears in your browser you can either click a 'Like' or 'Dislike' button on the toolbar, and in doing so your vote is then aggregated with all the other votes for that site and affects how often the site appears to other stumblers in future.

In terms of traffic generation StumbleUpon can be very effective in getting high levels of traffic, although in my own tests I've found the quality of the traffic to be quite low; i.e. lots of visitors, but very poor conversions, probably because people who 'Stumble' are mostly looking for entertainment and not necessarily looking for a product or service (or information relating to a problem or opportunity). However, maybe it'll work well for you and your target audience.

Get leverage on MyBlogLog

MyBlogLog is a community site primarily to help bloggers find other bloggers with similar interests. It can be used to increase traffic to your own blog and website. You will need to be running your own blog in order to sign up. Visit www.MyBlogLog.com to open your free account. Once you've applied for an account you'll be able to start using it to drive traffic. In this respect there are quite a few different techniques for driving traffic from *MyBlogLog*, but one of the most common ways is to add yourself to the 'Communities' of other *MyBlogLog* users, add them as a friend, then send them a comment. A percentage of your comments will result in reciprocal comments and generate traffic.

Some people report great results with using sites like *MyBlogLog* to generate traffic. The main issue I have with it is the potentially very low return on investment for the time you spend surfing for and joining *MyBlogLog* communities and leaving and replying to comments. However, as with any of the traffic tactics in this book, it could be that for *your* target audience and industry *MyBlogLog* works very well and may be worth testing.

Participate on Q&A sites

Yahoo Answers (http://answers.yahoo.com/) and LinkedIn Answers (www.linkedin.com/answers) are just two of a growing number of websites that allow visitors to post questions for the website's other visitors to answer. As a way of generating traffic to your site, you can search for people asking questions on topics *within your area of expertise*. When you submit your answer, it could include links to specific pages on your website, and result in targeted traffic. The key is to be one of the first to answer the question, and to provide a great answer that makes people notice your expertise and click the links to your site.

Join Ecademy, LinkedIn and other business specific social sites

Ecademy (www.Ecademy.com) and *LinkedIn* (www.LinkedIn.com) are just two bigger examples of the dozens, if not hundreds (or maybe even thousands) of sites where business people congregate for networking and online collaboration. Those sites have massive traffic, so if you open an account and join in on their online community discussions, a percentage of the people who see your participation will click through to your own website. There are many other ways you can gain traffic from these kinds of sites, but like anything, the first step is to always to sign up and get involved.

Build a Facebook following

Facebook (www.Facebook.com) is a global phenomenon now. Chances are you've already heard about it, and maybe even one of the hundreds of millions of people who use it on a daily basis to keep in touch. There are so many ways to get traffic from *Facebook* it would fill an entire book to cover them all, so for the sake of brevity I'll give you five ways you can drive traffic from it…

1) Sign up and create an interesting profile.

2) Invite friends, colleagues, business partners, prospects and active customers and clients to become a supporter of your *Facebook* presence.

3) Post regularly with interesting useful content, and seed your Facebook content with links back to your main website.

4) Support other Facebook users and comment on their Wall.

5) Start a 'Facebook Group' and build your own community of people interested in a topic related to what you sell.

Like I said, there are many other ways to drive traffic from *Facebook*—including having your own *Fanpage* and running paid adverts—but you should get a lot of traction from just those five to start with.

Participate on industry forums

In the same way as commenting on blogs can drive traffic, participating in industry forums can greatly increase your website traffic too. People who read and appreciate your comments will also be exposed to the links in your 'forum signature'—the block of text you can have added automatically to the bottom of each comment you post on the forum. Most forums also let you create a profile which includes links to your website.

Finding forums is easy. Search for the phrase "INDUSTRY forum" and replace the word INDUSTRY with whatever your industry is. You could even be more specific or 'lateral' in your searches and include more specific phrases in your searches.

One word of caution with this tactic: Be aware of how much time you spend commenting on forums and track how much traffic that 'time investment' sends to your site. Always ask—*Is it working and worth the time?*

Authority site reviews

Asking other people to review your products and services can be a very effective way of driving traffic to your sites if they agree to publish the review on their website which already gets massive traffic. I understand author *Tim Ferris* used this tactic to get massive traffic and exposure for his book 'The Four Hour Workweek.' He posted the book off to well-known and heavily visited blogs that were already speaking to his target audience. Many of those sites reviewed his book on their blog and created staggering levels of worldwide exposure entirely for free. The book ultimately became an International best-seller.

Perhaps sending off a free copy of your product or giving a free trial of your service could also get massive industry exposure and result in huge website traffic. If that doesn't work then you could try the alternative option which is to look for websites that offer to post reviews in return for a payment or 'reward' of some kind.

Perform e-mail marketing

Sending e-mails to your own 'house list' of email addresses—that's people whose email addresses you've got stored in a database you own—is one of the fastest sources of qualified, targeted web site traffic. With a click of a mouse you can send a single email message to hundreds or even thousands of your customers, clients and prospects. Each email can be personalised with each recipients name and other personal information. And best of all, include links in your emails, to pages on your website, and—provided your doing your email marketing effectively—you're almost **guaranteed** to get instant traffic and sales.

Email Marketing is *such* an important subject in terms of website traffic generation that I wrote a book about it!

In *this* book I'll briefly explain email marketing to give you an idea of what it's all about, but I strongly recommend you get hold of *Email Marketing Dynamite*, and put it *all* into practice at your earliest convenience. Until you do, your website won't be getting anywhere *near* as much traffic as it could!

To get a free download and also a free paperback copy of *Email Marketing Dynamite* visit **www.EmailMarketingDynamite.com**

So the two key ways in which you can perform email marketing are through email autoresponders, and email broadcasting.

Set up some Autoresponders

Autoresponder messages are a series or sequence of emails that you've written *in advance*, which are *automatically* delivered to your prospects after they've signed up to your email newsletter or filled in a form on your website.

From the recipient's perspective, autoresponders provide immediate gratification. For example, if someone visits your website and requests some free information from you, the autoresponder automatically emails them the information immediately, rather than having to wait for you to manually email it when you're next in the office.

Autoresponders allow you, the business owner, to maintain contact with many hundreds of thousands of prospects automatically. They also enable you to track responses to various offers, to assist you in your on-going marketing efforts.

Perhaps one of the biggest benefits of an autoresponder— in terms of driving traffic—is that every single email you stack into your autoresponder software can have **links back to your website.**

This means that when someone is added to your autoresponder sequence, they can automatically receive emails over the subsequent weeks, months or years that contain links encouraging them to revisit your website. *This is an* **extremely powerful** *way of ensuring your traffic remains constantly high.*

There are quite a few different kinds of autoresponder sequences you should consider writing;

1) Write a sequence of emails that go to **prospects** encouraging them to buy from you for the first time.

2) Write an autoresponder sequence that goes to **new customers.** Commonly referred to as a 'Stick Campaign', the purpose of your new customer autoresponder sequence is to mitigate 'Buyer's Remorse'—to make sure that the new customer is happy with their purchase, and secondly, to upsell and cross-sell them additional, related products and services.

3) Write a sequence of emails to go to **lapsed customers** or clients— people who have stopped buying from you. Your sequence could contain a special offer encouraging them do buy from you again.

4) Write a sequence of emails to go to **people you meet at conference and exhibitions,** to automatically nurture the relationship.

5) Write a sequence of emails to encourage **strategic alliances partners and affiliates** to get them to promote your products and services more, and provide them with extra resources and advice on how to promote more effectively.

Each one of those sequences can have links in them, back to your website, automatically getting people to revisit your web pages, automatically keeping traffic levels high.

Send an E-Mail Broadcast

Whereas email autoresponders are pre-written emails that go out to individuals who sign up to your email newsletter or fill in a website form to request information, or buy a product or service, *email broadcasting* instead refers to 'one off' emails that are simultaneously received by hundreds or thousands of your email subscribers at the same time.

You can use broadcasting, for example, to alert your subscribers to upcoming events, offer them 'early bird discounts', let them know when your seasonal sales are starting (or coming to a close), announce special offers or discounts and so on.

Ask Strategic Alliance Partners to Email For You

If you successfully form some strategic alliances, then they will hopefully agree to email their 'house lists' with links to your website. It's one of the fastest ways I know of to get massive traffic to any website. Just imagine if you have an alliance partner with a highly responsive list of more than 100,000 names and email addresses, of people who are *your* prospective customers and clients. If they send even just a single email to that list you could suddenly find a very large surge in traffic to your site. *Get ready for it!*

Get co-registration opt-ins

Co-registration refers to arrangements between two or more companies to share contact details as people sign up through a web form. To do this ethically, both companies should have an offer on the web form, explaining that when the visitor enters their details they receive free information from both companies, and also receive emails from both companies in future. One key advantage of co-registration is that both companies can share the cost of promoting the offer. Also, if both companies have a decent industry profile then they both benefit from each other's brand awareness.

An alternative to the standard approach to co-registration mentioned above, is where a company displays a separate check-box in an email sign-up form, where the user can opt-in to receive messages from a third-party. For example, a magazine running a contest may include a check-box for registrants to accept emails with future announcements from them, and also from the prize sponsor of the contest.

Set up walk-sort mail drops

If you have prospective customers in a particular geographic area, you can promote your products and services via leaflets, letters or postcards. To make this viable, ensure you have a very compelling offer that will entice people to respond immediately. And of course, one of the ways in which they can respond could be online at your website.

Add links to your email signature

You can configure your email software to automatically add what's called a 'signature' to the bottom of every email you send anyone. People generally use these to automatically include their name and job title. However, you can also add links to your websites, and if you also include with those links a call to action (maybe offer them a free report) then all of a sudden responses you give to general email enquiries may end up building your website traffic.

Offer & perform affiliate marketing

Affiliate marketing programmes are revenue-sharing arrangements set up by companies selling products and services. As an individual you could join another companies affiliate program, send them traffic and get paid if any of the traffic you send to their web pages purchases anything.

Variations of affiliate marketing include 'rewards sites', where users are rewarded with cash or gifts for the completion of an offer and the referral of others to the site.

In terms of using an affiliate programme to increase your own website traffic you'll need to start running your own affiliate programme.

Affiliates often use regular advertising methods. Those methods include organic search engine optimisation, paid search engine marketing, e-mail marketing, and sometimes display advertising. They also publish reviews of products or services offered by the affiliate.

Set up your own 'in-house' Affiliate Program

When someone agrees to participate in your affiliate programme, you reward them for sending people to your website, who in turn become customers. Customers are sent to your site through links on your associates' or affiliates' web sites. By developing and offering this type of programme, you generate increased business and increased links to your site and increased link popularity for search engines.

There are hundreds probably even thousands of affiliate services and software packages. Here are a few I've used in the past...

- www.iDevAffiliate.com
- www.InfusionSoft.com

Out-sourcing your Affiliate Programme

Setting up and running your own in-house affiliate programmes can take time and money and can be an extra burden. So an alternative option is to outsource your affiliate marketing programme and use third-party services to provide all the functionality and technical support and end-user assistance. Examples of these include…

- www.Tradedoubler.com

- www.AffiliateFuture.com

- www.AffiliateWindow.com

- www.ClickBank.com

One of the bigger advantages of using services like that is that, in most cases, *they already have massive traffic.* By using their service you're tapping into their existing user base of people looking for products and services they can promote for a commission.

And of course, if an affiliate on one of those sites successfully promotes and gets you new customers, those customers are then in your database and then become 'recycled traffic' back to your websites.

Ask for referrals

Research has proven that people who are referred to a business tend to spend more money—probably because people refer others who are highly qualified. When a friend or colleague tells you about a business you transfer the trust you have in the friend or colleague to the company, even if you've never heard of them before.

With this in mind, you could make asking your existing clients for referrals a part of your procedures for anyone involved in your sales or customer service departments. Referrals are an inexpensive method of capturing new, highly qualified clients, and a great way of increasing your website traffic.

You can offer gifts in return for referrals, or gifts to new prospects so your clients will be more likely to give you referrals. You can use direct mail, email, gift certificates your clients can pass on to prospects, even a business card with a great offer on the back. All of these aids make it far easier to capture low cost, high quality referrals.

And here's the key to using referrals to generate website traffic—the gifts and incentives you offer people to get them to refer for you could be collected online. And the gifts and incentives you offer the people they're referring to you could also be collected online, from your website. Do that, and you've just added another two powerful ways of increasing your website traffic.

Tell-a-Friend

Tell-a-Friend facilities allow your website visitors to easily recommend your website to their friends and colleagues. Here's how the more common Tell-a-Friend facilities work…

1) Your website visitor fills out a form on your website with both their own name and email address and also the names and email addresses of the people they're recommending your site to, and click a button to submit the form.

2) The Tell-a-Friend facility automatically sends a pre-written email message to all of the people whose details they provided, but with the name of the referrer (the person who filled in the Tell-a-Friend form) also in the email to prove it's not 'spam' and that the message is from someone they know.

3) One or more of the 'friends' who receive the email click a link and end up on the original website.

4) Finally, the more advanced Tell-a-Friend programmes that are available online send the referral a *reward* for successfully referring people to the website. (The reward could be a free download or other kind of incentive which is valuable to the receiver and can be sent to them instantly and automatically, but which doesn't actually cost you anything to fulfil.)

In my experience it's offering a reward that makes all the difference between a Tell-a-Friend facility being used or ignored.

One of the more advanced scripts I've used is Viral Friend Generator available from www.ViralFriendGenerator.com. It can even be configured to send *bigger* rewards to people who successfully refer larger numbers of their friends and colleagues. At the time of writing it costs around $97, but also note there are a lot of other Tell-a-Friend scripts available online, many of which are free, (although perhaps not as full featured as Mike's script.)

> NB: Some people misunderstand the way Tell-a-Friend scripts work and think that in some way it's 'spamming' the recipients (the 'friends'). That's not the case *provided* you use one of the more 'ethical' Tell-a-Friend scripts which *don't* store the 'friends' names and email addresses. The only way the friends email addresses should be added to the website owner's mailing list is if the referred friends click the link in the email they receive and personally visit the website and buy, enquire or subscribe. If they ignore the 'Recommendation email' from their friend then nothing else should happen.

E-Mail this Web page

A more simple alternative to adding a Tell-a-Friend facility to your site is to simply display links on your web pages that when clicked open an email window in their own email software, with a pre-written message in the subject line to the effect "Check out this website… www.website.com". Then the person who clicked the link simply adds their own comments to the email and clicks send. Any web developer with even basic programming skills should be able to add this type of facility to your web pages for very little cost.

Forward this Email

You could add a paragraph to the bottom of your emails that asks your email newsletter subscriber to forward it to any friends or colleagues they think may also be interested in the content.

Ask for Referrals Offline

Using your website to stimulate and encourage online referrals is a highly effective way of boosting your website traffic. Other ways of asking for referrals, as a way of driving website traffic, include asking customer or clients at face to face meetings if they'd refer you. If they say yes, guide them onto your Tell-a-Friend web page and help them fill it in with the details of, for example, three or more people they believe will also benefit from your product or service.

You could also send direct mail to existing customers and clients solely to ask them for referrals, and give them the address of a web page where they can do that and be *instantly rewarded* with a free gift or buying credits or some other type of incentive. Also consider including referral cards with your products, with the same kind of incentive—instant online rewards.

Ask for traffic at Face to Face meetings

If you've just had a great face to face meeting with a customer or client, how about walking them onto your Tell-a-Friend web page and helping them fill it in with the details of 3 or more people they believe will also benefit from your product or service.

Use Direct Mail to Get Online Referrals

Send your existing customers and clients a letter asking them for referrals, and give them a web address to submit them.

Call waiting and answer-phone messages

Update the *recorded telephone message* that plays to people who phone your office when you're not there. Instead of just asking them to "leave a message after the tone", also suggest they visit your website for the latest news, information and special offers (whatever's relevant for your business.) Also if they're calling your customer services or technical support phone number, the call queue message could suggest they visit your website to get answers to common questions.

Also your out of hours answer-phone message could have an extra call to action, giving callers compelling reasons to visit your website—seasonal special offers being one such example.

Enhance your compliment slips

More prominently, display your web address and provide a compelling call to action and all of a sudden the lowly compliment slip could be a source of new website traffic.

Train your Complaints dept.

Surprising to some, but your complaints department could become a source of web site traffic. You could train people who deal with complaints to issue online gift coupons and discount codes along with their apologies. In addition to this, your complaints staff could talk the caller onto a special area of your website if they've misunderstood a product or services function or utility. You could ask if they want to be signed up to your free online newsletter "worth £XXX a year", and you could also add them to a 'complaints' autoresponder sequence that automatically follows the complainer up in 'x' days or weeks to ensure they're satisfied with the remedial action taken. And of course, the email can contain links to relevant pages on your website, including feedback forms, more special/discount offers, or even "Refer a Friend" which you can ask them to fill in if they're happy with how to problem was resolved.

Start a loyalty programme

Rewarding and therefore encouraging loyal buying behaviour is a great thing for any company to systematically build into their marketing efforts. Start a loyalty programme and build into it various incentives to get customers and clients to return to your website, and refer other businesses, contacts, colleagues, friends, to the site too—by providing redeemable discount codes, bonus gifts, special deals, and early bird price offers.

Some of the World's biggest and fastest growing companies put a lot of emphasis and investment into their loyalty programmes, including integration with their website related marketing activities.

Send birthday, Christmas and anniversary cards and emails

Engage potential customers by letting them know they're important to you. For example, send them birthday greetings by email (see the example below), or even better, a proper printed birthday card with an offer for a special 'birthday discount'. You can of course do the same with Christmas, Easter and Anniversaries too.

Figure 5: Birthday email with a discount voucher

Start a print newsletter or magazine

Printed newsletters and magazines can have a more targeted readership than newspapers, and are generally read more thoroughly. They also have a longer life span and the print is higher-quality. Many magazines offer a classified ads or directory section at reasonable rates.

So, if you don't already publish one, consider starting an either paid or free physical (printed) monthly, bi-monthly or quarterly newsletter or magazine. Not only would that be a very powerful way to maintain top of mind awareness with your prospects and active customers and clients and increase your posture and industry profile, it also would be a regular opportunity to boost website traffic by seeding the entire publication with links to your site.

The disadvantages are that your production costs may be higher, and as many magazines and journals are published monthly, there's usually a longer lead time so you need to plan further in advance. However, they could be a very effective route to increasing your website traffic.

Get leverage at the Point Of Sale

Use eye-catching or attention-grabbing promotional material and display it at the point of sale (where purchases are made) to encourage people to visit your website too.

Ask for Email Addresses

Can you ask your customers for their email address at the point of sale? For most retail establishments like shops and restaurants I'd say there's a huge opportunity. Providing you can give your customers a good 'reason why' you want their email address, many will agree to it. Then you can start emailing them and encouraging them to click through to your website.

Till Receipts

A lot of people read (check) their till receipts, so do include your web site details and a compelling call to action as well as your other contact details on them.

Coupons

Give customers discount coupons which they can redeem online.

Start a petition

Conduct an online petition to gather new leads and get publicity for your business. Promote the petition on your industry forum and key web sites.

Encourage file sharing (P2P)

Take advantage of people's interest in watching and sharing online videos by uploading content your target audience want. Make sure your video contains your keywords. Provide links to your web site (or landing page).

Become a 'Cool Site of The Day'

If your web site is interesting or useful then you could consider submitting it to www.CoolSiteOfTheDay.com. If your site is featured it'll almost instantly get massive traffic. The caveat is they almost definitely won't feature your site if it's the usual type of corporate website. However, if you combine this tactic with other Massive Traffic tactics such as 'Creating a Free Online Tool' you could certainly stand a chance of getting featured on Cool Site of The Day. And there are many other types of similar 'cool' sites. Google the phrase "Cool Site of The Day" for a current list.

Create a free online tool or resource

If you've got an idea for a free software tool your prospects could use, see if you can find someone to turn it in to a special website. (Try sites like www.Elance.com or www.VWorker.com). Not only could your free tool site go viral (see Viral Marketing tactic), but everyone who uses it is a *qualified prospect*—and should be exposed to links to your other websites.

Two great examples of this...

- www.SplitTester.com — is a free online tool designed by Google Adwords gurus *Perry Marshall* and *Howie Jacobson*. It tells you whether your Adwords adverts have achieved something called statistical significance. Visit this site and you'll not only get the free use of a great tool, you'll also be exposed to links to their other websites and products and services.

- www.LifetimeValueCalculator.com — is a free online tool I created to help marketers determine their customer (or client's) average lifetime value, which is essential knowledge for anyone wanting to maximise customer or client acquisition and grow their business faster. People who visit this site also see and click links to my own range of products and services.

- www.HeadlineMachine.com — this site is still in development at the time of writing, but should hopefully be live by the end of August/September 2010. The concept is that with a few simple inputs this free tool will *automatically generate thousands of headlines* you can use on your websites, in your sales letter, brochures and emails... basically *anywhere* you need to get a reader to take action and buy enquire or subscribe. Again, people who use this site will see links and click through to my other websites.

What can *you* launch as a free online tool?

Accountants could create financial tools. Car leasing companies could create quote calculators. Dieticians could create meal planning tools. Letting agents could create tools to help landlords plan their rental rates, and so on. Be creative, create something highly useful, promote it using the other 207 Massive Traffic tactics and see how much traffic it attracts and diverts onto your other websites.

Buy sites that *already* get a lot of traffic

If you want instant traffic, one of the fastest ways is to simply buy a website (domain) that's *already* getting lots of traffic. There are websites that specialise in selling existing domains, where the price is based on a number of factors.

These factors include…

- *PageRank*—a score based on how 'important' Google thinks the domain is.

- *Age*—how long ago it was first registered. As a rule of thumb the older and more established a domain is, the more it costs.

- *Backlinks*—Domains that have lots of other third-party websites linking to them cost more money than sites that don't have any other website linking to them.

- *Domain name*—Some domains sell for hundreds or thousands of pounds simply because they're short and memorable.

- *Extension*—.com domain names usually cost more than .co.uk domains for example.

- *Reasons for sale*—If the seller wants 'fast cash' then you may be able to buy it for less money than it'd normally cost.

- *Traffic*—It stands to reason, a domain that's already getting ten thousand visitors a month is going to cost a lot more money than one that's getting only a few dozen visitors a month.

- *Conversion rate*—If the website is already selling a lot of products or generating many enquiries, it'll cost more than a site that's not producing any results.

How to find domains to buy

There are hundreds if not thousands of companies who specialise in buying and selling domain names and existing websites. These include…

- http://for-sale.domaintools.com/
- http://marketplace.digitalpoint.com
- http://www.domaining.com/
- http://www.namepros.com/

For an extended and current list of places to buy and sell domains go to Google and search on phrases like "buy old domains".

Write a book!

This is my third book, so from experience I can tell you that writing and publishing a book is an almost *guaranteed* way of generating more website traffic. Each time I launch a new book, the buzz and word of mouth it generates drives more traffic to my website. Also, the website links *in* my books are a source of targeted traffic. People read the book, see the links, and visit the site.

The common objection I usually get when I suggest this tactic is "I could never write a book, I just don't have the time!". Well, if you're thinking that then I'd urge you to visit the following link. It may be quite revealing!

➜   http://www.edrivis.com/general-strategy/become-a-published-author-in-less-than-7-days/

Summary—A Final Call to Action!

Traffic is the lifeblood of any website. Without traffic, your website is incapable of generating sales or enquiries. So my aim with this book was to make you aware of—and arm you with—as many effective traffic tactics as you need to make your online web marketing strategy hugely successful.

So, now you have more than 208 ways to drive more traffic, all you need to do is *implement* them!

Take massive action, *get massive traffic.*

Execute as many of the tactics *that are relevant to your business* as possible, and watch what happens as the floodgates open and a constant stream of new and repeat visitors washes over your site, time and time again.

I wish you every success in driving **massive** *traffic to your website.* Send an email to edrivis@strategicwebprofits.com and let me know what happens. I look forward to hearing of your success.

All my best,

Ed Rivis, August 2010.

P.S. Hopefully you're already signed up to receive email updates from me, but if not I'd urge you to register right now—by signing up for emails from me I'll be able to keep you updated with the latest innovations in website traffic generation. You can sign up via my blog at www.EdRivis.com.

GET MASSIVE TRAFFIC X4

In this book you've discovered more than 208 ways to drive traffic to your website. If you're feeling overwhelmed, *I don't blame you!* If you personally try and implement *all* these tactics you could be very busy for a *very* long time. Even if you try and *outsource* everything, you could be kept very busy trying to find and train people to do this all on your behalf, let alone monitoring the results they get for you.

So, the good news is that you only have to do just *four* of the tactics in this book to get massive traffic!

Using *Google Adwords, article marketing, traditional advertising and strategic alliances* you really *can* attract hundreds, or thousands or even hundreds of thousands of visitors to your website within as little as 24 hours... *guaranteed!*

Of course the key is to not just perform those four tactics, but to perform them *effectively*. For this reason I've created a special training programme to show you *exactly* how I and my private clients get massive traffic from just those four tactics. It's called **MASSIVE TRAFFIC X4** and it'll show you how to *open the floodgates to more visitors and more sales and profits.*

You can get more information at **www.MTX4.com**

Massive Traffic